A2 ...ge

Mo... ...ure

Susan Cockcroft

Seri... ...rth

Philip Allan Updates
Market Place
Deddington
Oxfordshire
OX15 0SE

Orders

Bookpoint Ltd, 130 Milton Park, Abingdon, Oxfordshire, OX14 4SB
tel: 01235 827720
fax: 01235 400454
e-mail: uk.orders@bookpoint.co.uk
Lines are open 9.00 a.m.–5.00 p.m., Monday to Saturday, with a 24-hour message
answering service. You can also order through the Philip Allan Updates website:
www.philipallan.co.uk

© Philip Allan Updates 2006

ISBN-13: 978-1-84489-552-6
ISBN-10: 1-84489-552-1

This guide has been written specifically to support students preparing for the
AQA Specification B English Language and Literature Unit 5 examination. The
content has been neither approved nor endorsed by AQA and remains the sole
responsibility of the author.

Printed by MPG Books, Bodmin

Philip Allan Updates' policy is to use papers that are natural, renewable
and recyclable products and made from wood grown in sustainable forests.
The logging and manufacturing processes are expected to conform to the
environmental regulations of the country of origin.

A2 English Language & Literature

Contents

Introduction

About this guide 4

Studying English Language and Literature at A2 4

Unit 5: key concepts 5

Assessment objectives 6

The examination 7

Tips for Unit 5 11

■ ■ ■

Content Guidance

About this section 14

Overview 15

Addressing Question 1 29

Addressing Question 2 37

■ ■ ■

Questions and Answers

About this section 48

Question 1: English drama pre-1770 49

Question 2: unseen texts 65

Introduction

About this guide

The aim of this unit guide is to help you prepare for the **Unit 5: Talk in Life and Literature** examination. It is intended as a revision aid, not a textbook. There are three sections to this guide:

- **Introduction** — this outlines the content of Unit 5, explains the format of the examination paper and places it within the context of the AQA (B) English Language and Literature A2 specification. It explains how you are assessed, gives you advice on how to prepare for the examination, and what procedure to follow in the examination.
- **Content Guidance** — this provides a guide to the key concepts you need to understand, the strategies you need to adopt and the approaches you need to apply in order to be successful in this unit. It also identifies ways in which you can write more successful answers, and shows you what pitfalls to avoid. There is detailed advice on how to prepare most effectively for this examination, thus increasing your confidence.
- **Questions and Answers** — this includes a detailed analysis of the format of both Questions 1 and 2, with explanations of what the examiner is looking for in response to each question. There is also an illustrated explanation of the mark scheme and the principles on which it is based. Examples of A- and C-grade answers are provided, accompanied by examiner comments that highlight the strengths and weaknesses of each answer and suggest ways of improving performance in each instance.

Studying English Language and Literature at A2

Having completed the AS English Language and Literature units, you are now ready to learn to apply more sophisticated linguistic and literary approaches to texts. The transition from AS to A2 presents different challenges in each unit; in Unit 5 the focus is on talk in real life and the way it is represented in literature.

You have already studied spoken language in all its variants in Unit 1 and you have learnt to recognise and differentiate a wide range of literary genres and sub-genres. You are now well prepared to 'raise your game' as you move into A2. Unit 5 enables you to discover:

- how to recognise the ways in which pre-1770 dramatists (including Shakespeare) achieve particular effects by their use of *dialogue* (Question 1)
- how to analyse and compare transcribed extracts of spontaneous conversation with passages of crafted 'literary' dialogue or monologue (Question 2)

What skills and knowledge do you need to be successful in this unit? First, for Question 1 you have to *know your set text* (i.e. the play your centre has chosen to study). Later in this guide you will find out about strategies for building up a secure and detailed knowledge of this play, so that no examiner can catch you out. Second, in addition to this textual confidence, you must have a good understanding of how spontaneous conversation works in both formal and informal contexts. You need to be able to recognise and interpret the patterns and conventions of talk in everyday conversation, and apply this understanding, not only to contemporary transcribed speech, but also to all literary representations of speech, whether in drama, fiction or poetry.

All this may seem a tall order — but many candidates do manage it successfully. If you work through this unit guide carefully, you can be just as successful. In addition, the skills and understanding you acquire will stand you in good stead for the future.

Unit 5: key concepts

Although both parts of this examination (Questions 1 and 2) focus on spoken language in life and literature, the emphasis is different in each question.

Question 1 focuses on the genre of drama, and the way in which pre-eighteenth-century dramatists exploit certain aspects and features of naturally occurring (spontaneous) speech to create particular dramatic effects. Your centre has chosen a set text from a range of options, including plays by Shakespeare and other seventeenth- or eighteenth-century dramatists.

Question 2 asks you to explore the way in which writers of different literary genres (fiction and poetry as well as drama) craft everyday speech for their own purposes by comparing spontaneous talk with crafted dialogue or monologue in a similar context.

The **key concepts** covered by this unit are explained below. They have different degrees of relevance to Questions 1 and 2, but all have fundamental relevance to the unit as a whole. These key concepts are: **discourse**, **context**, **genre**, **function**, **audience** and **dramatic effect**.

- **Discourse** — in the context of this unit, the term is used to describe spoken language and the conventions and patterns of spoken exchange (e.g. turn-taking, question–answer structures, modes of address etc.). It can also be applied to an extended passage of written or spoken language (i.e. longer than a sentence or paragraph). The term can also refer to the written or spoken language of different social, professional or interest groups (i.e. the discourse of education, the discourses of journalism or politics, the discourse of feminism, the discourse of climate change). For the purposes of this unit, discourse will be used to refer to the conventions and structures of *spoken* language.
- **Context** — this refers to the physical, social and/or psychological situation in which real people are talking (transcript extracts in Question 2), or in which characters are speaking to each other (literary extracts in Question 2). For example, a motorist stopping to ask a pedestrian for directions is a recognisable situation or context; a comparable literary context is the scene in Charlotte Brontë's novel *Villette*, where the heroine arrives in a foreign city without friends, and is given directions by a fellow traveller who knows the city. The *common context* here is being lost and needing help.

- **Genre** — this means a text type (either spoken or written), and there are numerous variants or sub-genres in each broad category. For example, the novel is a *written* literary genre with many sub-genres (including crime, science fiction, romantic fiction, historical fiction, fantasy etc.). Examples of *spoken* genres include everything from an interview to a sports commentary or a service encounter (i.e. buying bread or visiting the bank). Genre is particularly important in Question 2.
- **Function** — this can refer to the *purposes* of the speakers in a spontaneous exchange, to the purposes of a writer in crafting dialogue, or to the inner motivation of characters as they address each other in a play, novel or poem. Because all written and spoken language, literary and non-literary, has a range of functions, this concept is highly relevant to Unit 5 overall. It is mentioned specifically in Question 2.
- **Audience** — this refers to all those listening or taking part in a spontaneous conversation. It also refers to readers of literary genres, and to people listening to and/or watching a performance. It is crucial that you keep in mind that every piece of spoken or written language is addressed to an audience, whether this audience is physically present or not.
- **Dramatic effect** — this relates particularly to Question 1 and refers to the way an audience's responses are manipulated by the dramatist's particular use of certain literary, linguistic or rhetorical strategies.

Assessment objectives

As you work through this unit guide, you can use the assessment objectives (AOs) listed below and on p. 7 to check that your draft answers are on the right lines. However, there is no need to worry about remembering them yourself. It is the question-setter's responsibility to ensure that the AOs are built into the format of the questions. A relevant and detailed answer to the question you have been set will automatically fulfil the AOs.

One further point: each assessment objective has its own 'weighting' (i.e. proportionate importance). The AOs listed for Unit 5 have *equal* weighting, with the exception of AO3ii. This has *double* weighting because you are working at A2. AS students are expected to understand texts, whereas A2 candidates have higher-level skills, so they should be able not only to understand but also to *evaluate* texts and techniques.

Apart from this point, you should not find the descriptions of the assessment objectives difficult to follow, and you will probably be saying to yourself as you read them 'Yes, I'm doing that already'.

The Unit 5 specification has the following assessment objectives:

AO1	Communicate clearly the knowledge, understanding and insights gained from a combination of literary and linguistic study, using appropriate terminology and accurate written expression.

AO2ii	Respond with knowledge and understanding of texts of different types and from different periods, exploring and commenting on relationships and comparisons between them.
AO3ii	Use and evaluate different literary and linguistic approaches to the study of written and spoken language, showing how these approaches inform their readings.
AO4	Show understanding of the way contextual variation and choices of form, style and vocabulary shape the meanings of texts.
AO5	Identify and consider the ways attitudes and values are created and conveyed in speech and writing.

The examination

This unit is assessed by a written examination lasting 2 hours. There are two questions, each of which carries 35 marks. There are 70 marks available in total.

Both questions are compulsory. Question 1 must be answered with reference to whichever pre-1770 drama text you have studied, although the format of the question may vary slightly. Question 2 offers you a choice between two questions on different pairs of extracts, one non-literary and one literary.

To do as well as possible, you must answer both questions and allocate approximately the same amount of time (an hour) to each. Allow 10 minutes' reading and planning time before you start to write. This advice will not be unfamiliar to you — teachers always urge students to read and plan before writing, though in the anxiety of the exam situation candidates often do the very opposite.

Here are some dos and don'ts for Unit 5:

Don't...

- start writing immediately — but (just as importantly), don't struggle with making the first sentence perfect; you can always tweak it later
- write such a lengthy plan that you have no time to write the actual answer
- get carried away and forget the second question — use approximately the same amount of time for each question to achieve the maximum possible marks

Do...

- allow yourself time to read through the whole paper carefully
- jot down ideas as you read through the questions (you can write on the exam paper)
- make a *short* plan before you start to write (no more than a third of a side per question)
- link your plan with the actual question — don't rely on your memory of a past paper, look at what this question requires

Question 1

In this question, you are asked to look at two quite different passages from your set play and discuss the way in which spoken language and discourse conventions are used by the dramatist to create particular dramatic effects. A sample Question 1 is shown below.

---

1 English drama pre-1770

Read the **two** passages from the play you have studied.

Discuss the ways in which these **two** passages reveal the playwright's skills in producing specific dramatic effects.

In your answer you should consider:
- context (including *brief* reference to the play as a whole)
- spoken language features and discourse conventions
- literary, grammatical and rhetorical features
- phonological features including delivery of lines in performance
- any other relevant aspects

Approaching Question 1

The greatest advantage that you can have when answering Question 1 is a secure, detailed knowledge of the play (inside out, back to front, line by line). Moreover, if you have seen it in performance, whether on stage, film or in the classroom, you will recognise the two passages, identifying confidently the situation, characters and immediate context. A cool and thoughtful look at the exact wording of the question will then enable you to jot down ideas about each bullet point, as you start to explore the extracts in detail.

One well-worn but still useful strategy is to underline key words in the main question (i.e. 'ways', 'skills', 'reveal', 'dramatic effects'). Referring to these key words, you can then use the bullet points to focus your answer better.

Assuming that you do know your set play thoroughly, that you have recognised the passages and that you have read the question carefully, what more can be done to ensure success? Some suggestions are listed below.

- **Avoid generalisations in your introduction**
  — about 'Shakespeare the genius'
  — about modern 'everyday talk' and the relative absence of non-fluency features
  — about Shakespeare's other plays

- **Get to the point and focus immediately on the context of the passage**
  — what is happening *now* in this passage?
  — what happened just *before*?
  — what is going to happen just *after*?
  — how important is the passage to the play as a *whole*?

- **Consider each passage separately**
  — you have not been asked to compare the passages
  — comparison leads to important points about each passage being missed

- **Make sure you understand the meaning of 'dramatic effect'**
  — dramatic effects are planned and created by the playwright
  — dramatic effects are experienced by the audience
  — you need to be able to identify dramatic effects in your text
  — you must be able to explain how they work to affect the audience
  — it may help your argument to make brief reference to relevant linguistic theory

Question 2

In Question 2 you have to choose between two questions. Each consists of two sets of unseen texts (the question on each pair of texts will be broadly similar). Each pair will include an extract from a transcribed spontaneous exchange, and a crafted passage from fiction, poetry or drama. Because the major task in Question 2 is to *compare* the differences between spontaneous and crafted speech, the unseen passages in each option will be linked in some way. For example, they may share:
- a common *context* (e.g. a job interview, a railway journey)
- a common *purpose* (e.g. seeking directions, requesting a medical diagnosis)
- a similar *relationship* between speakers (e.g. mother and child, friends at university)
- a common *genre* (e.g. a monologue by female speaker)
- a similar *pattern of exchange* (e.g. a question-and-answer format)

Whether you take this examination in January or June, you can be confident that there will be a choice of literary genres to compare in Question 2. Remember that broad genres can include many sub-genres, so do not be thrown if there is some slight variation within the categories of novel, poem and play. For example, extracts from a verse play, a comic monologue or poetic prose would still be described as literary.

Question 2 consists of a brief contextualised description of each pair of extracts, followed by a statement of the task. Bullet points are provided to guide you through your answer. An example of Question 2a is shown below.

2a Unseen texts

Text A is an extract from a transcribed consultation between a doctor and a patient.

Text B is an extract from the novel *Middlemarch* (1872) by George Eliot. Mr Casaubon, an elderly scholar and clergyman, has requested a consultation with the doctor, Mr Lydgate. Dorothea is Mr Casaubon's young wife. Mr Casaubon fears that his ill health might interfere with the completion of his lifelong work.

Compare the two texts, commenting on the ways in which they reflect differences and similarities between talk in real life and talk in literature.

You should refer in your answer to:
- the significance of context and function
- the functions of interaction
- how attitudes and values are conveyed

The question is followed by the two extracts.

Approaching Question 2

As both texts for this question are unseen, you will have to allocate time from your hour to read the extracts attentively and decide which pair suits you better. Allow 10 minutes for this focused reading, but don't worry if it takes a little longer. Better to make a good choice, produce a short plan and write confidently for 40 minutes than start writing too soon, dither, change options and then be pushed for time. Thinking and planning carefully will bring their own reward.

When you read through the texts, make a note of any literary or linguistic features which strike you as interesting and different, and which can be fitted into your comparison. Don't forget that your main task is to *compare the ways in which talk is used* in both texts. Use the bullet points to help you focus your answer — but make sure you have looked at them carefully. They are not always the same.

Unlike the task in Question 1, in Question 2 you must *compare* the passages if you are to achieve a high mark.

You have now chosen your option, read the passages carefully, noted interesting features and points of comparison, and made a brief plan. What else can you do to write a better answer? The following general advice should be helpful.

- **Identify the context and genre of each passage**
  - focus on the two exchanges; what element do they have in *common*?
  - is the physical *situation* similar?
  - do the participants have a common *purpose* (e.g. to seek information)?
  - is the *genre* similar?

Once you have recognised what the passages have in common, it will be much easier to compare them and identify differences as well as similarities.

- **Identify the audience and purpose(s)**
  - in a spontaneous exchange, the audience consists of the speakers themselves (even though you are reading the transcript, you were not present at the exchange)
  - in a spontaneous exchange, the *speakers'* purposes are the only ones which count
  - in literary texts, the audience consists of interested adults (or possibly children)
  - in the genres of *poetry* and *fiction*, the writer is usually addressing a reading audience
  - in the genre of *drama* there are two potential audiences: a listening audience (which is present at a performance) and a reading audience (not present at a performance)
  - in any literary text the author will have very clear purposes (creating character, forwarding plot, describing atmosphere, conveying emotions or ideas or opinions)

- **Use the bullet points to structure your comparison of the two texts**
  — don't ignore the bullet points in the question — they are there to help you
  — don't simply describe each text or make generalisations about it
  — look for features to compare under each bullet point (e.g. discourse conventions, figurative language, grammatical, rhetorical or phonological features)
  — always provide textual support when making a point — this is essential

In unplanned speech, the participants themselves are responsible for what is said: in literature (whether poetry, drama or fiction) it is the author alone who is responsible for everything that the characters say.

Tips for Unit 5

- Know your set text thoroughly.
- Use your knowledge of spoken language and discourse theory with confidence.
- Read the passages in Question 1 slowly and carefully, as if looking at them for the first time. You may be surprised at how much you see.
- Always make sure you write on both passages in Question 1.
- Read the rubric of Question 2 carefully.
- Remember to spend 1 hour only on each question.

Finally, here is a mantra for success, applicable to both questions on the Unit 5 paper:
- **Identify** the language feature.
- **Explain** how it works.
- **Relate** it to the meaning and purpose of the passage.

Content
Guidance

This section covers the terms, concepts and skills relevant to both questions on the Unit 5 examination paper. Divided into three parts, it shows you how to make more effective use of this detailed knowledge.

The first part is an overview of a range of topics including spoken language and discourse theory, appropriate use of linguistic and rhetorical terminology, dramatic discourse, blank verse and poetic form, context, issues of audience, staging and performance, genre in literature and schema in talk.

The second part concentrates on Question 1; it explores interesting ways of studying pre-1770 texts and becoming comfortable with their rather different language. It also suggests ways of analysing dramatic texts and recommends not only revision strategies but also techniques to maximise the success of your exam answer.

The third part focuses on Question 2, and pays particular attention to increasing confidence in your transcript-reading skills, by exploring and understanding how and why transcripts are made. There is detailed discussion of the three basic literary genres, with a clear analysis of what authors are attempting to do in each genre when crafting spoken language for literary purposes. Finally, there is focused advice on how to construct a more effective comparison of texts within the framework provided by the bullet points in the exam question.

Overview

Spoken language and discourse

Understanding how spoken language works in everyday life, in all sorts of situations and between all sorts of people, is at the heart of Unit 5. Ever since you started to look at transcripts of speech or tape-recorded and transcribed conversations at AS, the importance and extraordinary variety of human spoken communication will have become clear to you. By the end of the A2 year you should have acquired a sophisticated awareness not only of individual speech features, but also of variations in people's fluency or non-fluency and why this happens. You will know about people's set expectations (schemas) of conversational exchanges in certain familiar (and sometimes unfamiliar) contexts. You will be able to recognise how the situation or context can make a huge difference to the way in which people speak to each other, and how personal factors affecting the participants can also make things different. You will also be 'tuned in' to recognise and understand patterns of spoken exchange and discourse conventions that most people are unaware of using in everyday life.

Your task in this unit is to be an observer, a detective, an artist or pattern seeker in spoken texts, both literary and non-literary. Learning something of the explanations and theories about spoken language proposed by experts (ranging from sociolinguists to discourse analysts) can be useful and you may want to apply some of this theory to the exam texts you are analysing. You may also find it helpful to understand how rhetoric is still alive and kicking today, not just in advertising but also in ordinary conversation, political debate and literature.

Using your knowledge of spoken language and discourse conventions

Start with the **macro** perspective (an overview):

- **Identify the purpose behind the speakers' talk. Are they:**
  - exchanging information?
  - expressing feelings?
  - being persuasive?
  - being friendly?
  - playing power games?
- **Decide how the exchange is working. Look for evidence first at the discourse level:**
  - are face needs being met?
  - are the Gricean maxims fulfilled?
  - is the schema familiar to the participants?
  - do the discourse conventions support the identified purpose?

Now look for evidence at the **micro** perspective (text level):

- **Examine:**
  - turn-taking practices
  - terms of address
  - use of discourse markers
  - normal non-fluency features
  - exchange structure
  - grammatical features
  - deixis
- **Consider** whether these features, conventions and patterns support your interpretation of the spoken text.

Examples from candidates' scripts

Example 1

The passage discussed in this answer is from Shakespeare's play *The Winter's Tale* (III.ii). It occurs during the trial scene, where Queen Hermione stands wrongly accused of adultery by her insanely jealous husband, King Leontes. Key words have been underlined.

> Leontes, in his confused state, only uses <u>declaratives</u>. He uses the <u>royal plural</u> 'our' in an attempt to <u>show</u> that it is not personal, and that this trial is being held for the good of the state. However, it is Hermione who uses <u>imperatives</u>: 'spare your threats!' 'Apollo be my judge.' Even though she is on trial, her innocence and purity give her the <u>power</u> in this scene.

The candidate uses knowledge of grammar to explain the emotional force of the passage. The queen is so confident of her innocence that she uses commands (imperatives) to her husband, the king, who is able only to make statements (declaratives) in response.

Example 2

This passage is part of a comparison between a doctor–patient exchange in real life and one in literature (see p. 9). Key words have been underlined.

> A big similarity between text A and text B is that they both have a <u>transactional</u> function, with both patients wanting to get the appointment done and see if they are OK. Text A is full of <u>non-fluency</u> features. There are <u>false starts</u>: 'What it is er I work with elderly people'. Most non-fluency features come from the patient, which could be expected from the context. He is trying to <u>clarify</u> and <u>explain</u> what is wrong with himself, which can be difficult to do. He could also be <u>nervous</u>, as some people do not like doctors. This is also a reflection of who has the <u>power</u> here.

The candidate has identified correctly that the transactional purposes of the real patient and the fictional patient are the same — they both want to get a diagnosis from their doctor. The real patient is nervous and the candidate links this with his use of non-fluency features such as hesitation.

Example 3

This is a comparison between young women talking over lunch in real life and in Jane Austen's novel *Pride and Prejudice*. Again, key words have been underlined.

> The participants in text C appear to be quite relaxed and the <u>good nature</u> of their relationship is <u>demonstrated</u> by their <u>interruptions</u> of each other's speech. Furthermore, <u>back-channel</u> behaviour in the form of <u>continuers</u> 'mm' and 'yeah'…are used to <u>demonstrate</u> that they are <u>listening</u> to each other <u>carefully</u>…In <u>contrast</u> to the relaxed feel of text C, the <u>excitement</u> of the characters in text D…can be deduced by analysing the <u>reporting clauses</u>…we are told that the characters are 'exclaiming' and crying out 'with the greatest satisfaction'.

The candidate argues that the real young women are such good friends that interrupting each other freely is a sign of intimacy and a relaxed mood; in contrast, Austen describes the conversation of the Bennett sisters (who actually know less about each other) as a more structured (if noisy) exchange.

Using theory to improve your answer

Since it became possible in the twentieth century for scholars to have ready access to recording equipment, research into spoken language in all its varieties has made huge strides. Many universities have substantial data banks (called 'corpora') that allow scholars to investigate the most complex patterns of spoken usage. The relevance of this explosion of knowledge to A-level students is obviously limited by practical considerations such as time and energy. You can, however, benefit from the research of others by becoming familiar with key research trends and discoveries. This enables you to support and enrich your own arguments in an essay with brief but pertinent references. It will also impress examiners.

Speech act theory

When a speaker (or character) makes a statement that has the power of action, it can be described as **performative** (e.g. *Othello:* 'I kiss thee ere I kill thee'). Speech act theory (Austin and Searle 1969) identifies spoken language as performing an act of communication (e.g. 'I congratulate you!'). Performative speech acts tend to convey a sense of power and purpose.

Conversational analysis

Be aware of how conversations are structured. Look at openings and closures, overlaps, latched talk, simultaneous speech and interruptions. Ask yourself the following questions:

- Who has the power in this conversation?
- Who has the longest turns, holds the floor for longest or refuses to allow topic shifts?

- Is the conversation you are studying (whether in real life or literature) about getting something done (**transactional**), or is it more of a personal chat (**interactional**)?
- What are the speakers trying to achieve — or what relationships are being revealed?
- Are there any adjacency pairs or three-part exchange structures?
- Are some speakers more or less fluent than others?
- Who uses hedges and what can we deduce about them or the context?
- How much use is there of deixis?
- Are there many discourse markers?
- Is the conversation collaborative and cooperative or not?

If you ask yourself these questions, you are undertaking conversational analysis (Sacks et al. 1984). Being able to see how an exchange is structured will help you to describe how it works, and being able to describe the function of an exchange shows competence and understanding.

Politeness theory

Politeness theory can refer to everything from addressing positive and negative face needs (Goffman 1981) to cooperative talk and the Gricean maxims of truth, relevance, appropriateness of style and length of turn (Grice 1975).

If you are looking at a crafted exchange in a play, for example, especially between people of differing status, you are likely to find examples of positive and negative politeness, such as terms of address, joke-making, apologising, seeking agreement, hedging or being indirect. These are used to give the audience a clearer sense of the characters involved.

In an unplanned, spontaneous exchange, you should be able to recognise people's face needs by the way they speak to each other. This should enable you to gauge the relative success of the exchange.

Being able to identify cooperative speech in a text will impress any examiner — providing you can explain the theory and give textual support. For example, in the doctor–patient exchanges discussed in example 2 (p. 16), the candidate went on to note the way in which both doctors addressed the face needs of their patients ('just relax back as best you can' or 'come and sit yourself down').

Narrative structure theory

People tell each other stories all the time, whether it is the funny thing that happened on the way home or a holiday anecdote. Indeed, listening to stories is a pleasure the youngest of children can enjoy. Labov's narrative structure theory derived from his analysis of adolescent oral narratives (1972) though it can be applied to written as well as spoken language. It is often illuminating to apply the sequence he describes (**abstract, orientation, complicating action, evaluation, resolution, coda**) to an unseen text, bearing in mind that these elements may not all be present.

Narrative in Question 1 could range from Othello's account of his youthful adventures, to the grim account of Antigonus' fateful encounter with the bear in *The Winter's Tale*. Being able to recognise narrative structure means that you can see how an author crafts conversation to develop a narrative, or how speakers talking together casually construct a shared narrative.

For example, in a transcribed account of a visit by the narrator to an unknown uncle in the Question and Answer section, her story of the visit follows Labov's principles.

Frame and schema theory

Theoreticians argue that we use past experiences to structure or 'frame' our use of discourse. We recognise familiar 'cues' or patterns, and adjust our speech to the appropriate 'frame', whether we are participating in a **transactional** exchange such as visiting the doctor or an **interactional** exchange such as gossiping with friends.

Tannen (1993) and Semino (1997) each developed these theories further. They suggested that such repeated experiences create not just a pattern of expectations, but an internalised 'mental model'. This mental model is called a **schema**, a term which is particularly useful in describing paired situations and contexts. You should refer to schemata in Question 2, where you are asked to compare unseen texts from real life and literature. Schema theory can help you to recognise the **schemata**, or matching elements, that the texts have in common. They may share common situations (scenes), purposes (plans and goals) or genres (scripts).

In June 2005, both pairs of texts had a common schema, as in Question 2a — consulting a doctor — and Question 2b — employer/employee negotiations.

A variation on the use of schema in literature can be seen in a play such as *A Midsummer Night's Dream*. The comedy of Titania falling in love with Bottom lies in the fact that her passionate devotion goes *against* audience expectations of romantic love.

Gender theory

The relationship between gender and language has engaged linguists' attention since the 1960s and it shows no signs of diminishing. Candidates often find this area of language study intriguing, but sometimes apply gender theory to spoken texts in an unbalanced way. For example, male as well as female spoken usage needs to be considered when analysing talk in the light of gender theory.

Furthermore, making an assumption that gender is the most important factor in a spoken exchange can lead to other equally significant factors (such as power) being ignored. For example, in the second act of Caryl Churchill's play *Top Girls* (1982), the businesswoman Marlene interviews a prospective female employee. Gender is not significant in the interview; what matters is the way power is weighted towards the employer, disempowering the interviewee. Churchill has crafted the exchange to reveal more about Marlene's character to the audience, with important implications for the play's development.

> MARLENE: Well, Jeanine, what's your present job like?
>
> JEANINE: I'm a secretary.
>
> MARLENE: Secretary or typist?
>
> JEANINE: I did start as a typist but the last six months I've been a secretary.
>
> MARLENE: To?
>
> JEANINE: To three of them, really, they share me. There's Mr Ashford, he's the office manager, and Mr Philby is sales, and —
>
> MARLENE: Quite a small place?
>
> JEANINE: A bit small.
>
> MARLENE: Friendly?
>
> JEANINE: Oh it's friendly enough.
>
> MARLENE: Prospects?
>
> JEANINE: I don't think so, that's the trouble.
>
> (From Question 2b, January 2003)

Marlene's short turns and barked-out questions make Jeanine immediately defensive and cause her to explain too much. The fact that both speakers are women is irrelevant — Jeanine's uncertainty, a trait often characterised as feminine, is much more to do with her feeling of disempowerment, in contrast with the empowered Marlene.

When you are looking at an unseen text (whether spontaneous or crafted) and wondering whether gender is a significant factor, do not assume that other factors are not equally, if not more, important. To focus only on the idiolect of female speakers, and to be unaware of male speech, is also unwise.

Although gender theory is more often cited in Question 2, a brief and relevant reference can often be helpful in answering Question 1. For example, in *Othello*, Shakespeare presents Desdemona as a complex character whose language ranges from the modest and deferential to sharply witty and forthright. The dramatic effect of this is to engage the audience's admiration and sympathy.

Language and power theory

No one expects A-level students to know about the complexities of discourse analysis theory. However, you may find Fairclough's (2001) work on language and power interesting and useful. He draws attention to the ways in which uneven power relations are expressed in interactions. For example, a senior doctor on a hospital round with medical students may interrupt and control their contributions to the interaction in various ways. Because he/she has greater knowledge and experience in the field of medicine, otherwise inappropriate disruptions of the exchange are accepted.

You will be familiar with other ways of asserting power in interactions, including agenda-setting, using longer turns than others, refusing to allow topic shifting or to give other speakers the floor. You may find it rewarding to consider power relations as part of your textual analyses in the examination.

Grammar

Being able to comment on grammatical features in a spoken text shows a confident understanding of the way speech works, as well as a recognition that written and spoken language often use different grammatical features and syntactic structures. This section describes a range of grammatical features which can be used by a speaker or writer to communicate meaning as well as to provide structure for utterances or sentences.

Don't think that you are expected to refer to all the grammatical features described below in a single answer. The purpose of this section is to give you a sense of some grammatical features that you may be able to identify and explain.

If you understand and can use the technical terms used below — fine. Look up any unfamiliar terms in the following sections well before the exam. However, explaining what is happening within the grammar of a text in *your own words* is just as useful.

Verbs

In any spoken text, whether it is crafted or spontaneous, verb forms are worth looking at closely. There are many more verbs than nouns in spoken language.

- Check the frequency and use of imperative, interrogative and declarative forms in your text — these are all linked with potential *assertion of power* between speakers/characters.
- Are the finite verbs mainly active? If not, what effect is being conveyed (is the subject being acted upon, failing to act or being *disempowered*)?
- Is there much use of modal auxiliaries (would, should, could, might, ought to), expressing differing degrees of *uncertainty*?
- Is the exchange full of factual *information* conveyed by transitive verbs, or description of scenes and events conveyed in a more open-ended way by intransitive verbs?
- Are present participles ('-ing' forms) used a lot to communicate *urgency*?
- What role does time (shown by verb tense) play in the text? Is the present tense used to describe past events with more *immediacy*? Is the future being described, and is it *certain* (simple future) or *uncertain* (conditional 'if...' clause)?
- Does it matter whether an action is completed or continuous (i.e. is aspect relevant)?

Pronouns

Personal and demonstrative pronouns occur frequently in spoken exchanges, and may be worth commenting on. For example, a *dominant personality* can be revealed by frequent use of 'I', 'we', 'me' and 'us'. Frequent deictic use of pronouns such as 'this', 'that', 'there' and 'here' helps to show the participant/audience's precise *location* and *context* (e.g. *Macbeth*: 'It this a dagger which I see before me,/The handle towards my hand?')

Syntax

It is useful to be aware of **syntax** — the patterns of language and the organisation or structure of both unplanned utterances and constructed conversations in crafted texts. For example, character and plot tension in literature can readily be expressed through length of sentence and level of syntactic complexity.

Thus, at moments of high drama, extended compound-complex sentences with many subordinate clauses are more likely to slow down than speed up the narrative. Rapid, short, simple utterances in spontaneous exchanges can often express tension, whereas more extended talk, uninterrupted by non-fluency features, conveys a relaxed mood. Incomplete sentences, phrases and clauses, accompanied by hesitations, repairs and hedges, reflect uncertainty in a speaker/character. In the passage from *Top Girls* (p. 20), Marlene's one-word utterances convey a staccato expression of dominance over Jeanine, the unfortunate interviewee.

In Question 1, the dramatist may use any of these syntactic features, discourse markers or non-fluency features to support characterisation or create particular dramatic effects — keep your eyes open for them. An example of grammatical and syntactical features adding dramatic force to an exchange can be seen in the passage below from *Twelfth Night*. This scene comes near the end of the play, when the confusion of mistaken identities is about to be resolved. Olivia, in love with the disguised Viola (known as Cesario), has married Viola's shipwrecked twin, Sebastian, thinking he is Cesario. Duke Orsino, unable to persuade Olivia to love him, is outraged that his young emissary, Cesario, has apparently betrayed him.

OLIVIA:	Where goes Cesario?
VIOLA:	After him I love More than I love these eyes, more than my life More by all mores than e'er I shall love wife If I do feign, you witnesses above, Punish my life, for tainting of my love!
OLIVIA:	Ay me, detested! How am I beguiled!
VIOLA:	Who does beguile you? Who does do you wrong?

OLIVIA:	Hast thou forgot thyself? Is it so long?
	Call forth the holy father! *(exit an attendant)*
ORSINO:	Come away!
OLIVIA:	Whither, my lord? Cesario, husband, stay!
ORSINO:	Husband?
OLIVIA:	Ay, husband. Can he that deny?
ORSINO:	Her husband, sirrah?
VIOLA:	No, my lord, not I.

Twelfth Night V.i.132–46

There are 16 short sentences in this extract, mainly composed of questions. The tension is increased by this rapid-fire sequence, and the use of imperatives and inter-rogatives creates an atmosphere of high emotion, including anger, bewilderment and passionate love.

Rhetoric: recognising persuasion at work

Rhetoric can be described as 'the art of persuasive discourse', or more simply, the art of persuasion. One of the earliest theorists of rhetoric was Aristotle (384–322 BC). He emphasised the relationship between rhetoricians and their audience (much early rhetoric was spoken, not written), describing rhetoric as a kind of **dialogue** between the persuader and the persuaded. Today this dialogue may be *spoken* (in law courts, parliament, television advertising) or *written* (in journalism, creative writing, advertising). Persuaders can draw on every language resource to make their case more effectively. Much of what this section has already considered could provide ammunition and support for the skilled persuader.

Some of the most frequent and successfully used rhetorical devices are listed below, with brief explanations. This should help you to identify rhetorical devices at work in texts. They are grouped under two broad headings: **tropes** and **schematic devices**.

Tropes

Tropes are associated with the use of the speaker's or writer's imagination to draw a comparison or to make a vivid picture for the audience. Some frequently encountered examples are:

- metaphor
- simile
- personification
- irony

- metonymy — based on association (e.g. 'the White House' is used to represent both the US president and his/her staff)
- synecdoche — a part is used to stand for the whole (e.g. 'there is a sail on the horizon' implies a whole ship is there)
- allegory — usually a story with a double meaning, often a subversive one

Schematic devices

Schematic devices are associated with patterns or structures in language which have particular focused effects. Examples include:

- hyperbole — exaggeration ('You're the greatest!')
- litotes — underplaying a situation deliberately ('Only a few million pounds left? You're really hard up, I can see!')
- antithesis — placing opposites together ('You see that her eyes are open? Ay, but their sense is shut': Lady Macbeth sleepwalking)
- listing or 'heaping-up' — accumulating a large group of words or phrases, creating a mass effect
- syntactic parallelism — clauses or phrases with exactly the same structure but with a different meaning ('Against all expectation, the criminal reformed; against all expectation, the victim offended')
- repetition — there are many variations of this, from single words and phrases to entire clauses
- build-up or incrementum — listing, with the final item listed making the climactic point
- triple structures — grouping words or phrases in threes, usually to emphasise a point
- rhetorical question — a familiar device, used to challenge the listener or audience in some way

Being aware of the frequency of rhetorical devices throughout spontaneous and crafted speech will alert you to the ways in which meaning is enhanced and persuasion increased. An example from *A Midsummer Night's Dream* shows a highly effective use of various rhetorical devices. The extract is from early in the play, when the lovers, Lysander and Hermia, have run away to avoid her forced marriage. Demetrius, Hermia's rejected lover, is seeking them in the woods, pursued by Helena, who is hopelessly in love with him.

DEMETRIUS:	Do I entice you? Do I speak you fair?
	Or rather do I not in plainest truth
	Tell you I do not nor I cannot love you!
HELENA:	And even for that do I love you the more.
	I am your spaniel; and, Demetrius,

> The more you beat me I will fawn on you
> Use me but as your spaniel: spurn me, strike me
> Neglect me, lose me; only give me leave,
> Unworthy as I am, to follow you.
>
> *A Midsummer Night's Dream* II.i.199–207

In line 1, Demetrius uses two **rhetorical questions** to express his angry exasperation. Helena's response is full of **hyperbole** as she compares herself with a cowed animal, and she uses **antithesis** ('beat me/fawn on you') as well as **incrementum** ('spurn me, strike me/Neglect me, lose me; only give me leave') to convey her obsessive love.

Making sense of sound patterning in texts

Because speech, whether spontaneous or crafted, is made up of sound, sound patterning is an important mode of communicating with an audience. However, speech is not sound alone, but sound that conveys meaning via words. Words are groupings of sounds to which speakers of a language assign arbitrary and agreed meanings. Our interest is in the ways ordinary people in conversation (or characters in dialogue) use sound patterning to enhance the communication of their meaning.

It will be no surprise that sound patterning was also part of the persuasive repertoire of the classical rhetorician. For example, not only would an orator's words be chosen carefully, but the way the speech was delivered was crucial. In other words, **performance skills** were as essential to a classical rhetorician as they are to any modern actor, who delivers his or her lines in the way the director, dramatist or producer thinks best.

Rhetorical theorists identified different sound patterning strategies, most of which you will be familiar with (though possibly unaware of their classical origins). Some examples are listed below:

- alliteration — repetition of initial (first) consonant in a group of words
- assonance — repetition of vowel sound in medial (middle) position
- dissonance — deliberately discordant sounds grouped together
- consonance — repetition of consonant in medial or final (end) position
- onomatopoeia — sound suggesting meaning of word
- puns and word play — same-sound or similar-sound repetition
- full rhyme or half-rhyme
- end-rhyme or end-stopping
- metrical variation — e.g. blank verse (iambic pentameter), ballad metre, refrain
- caesura — a break mid-line to emphasise change of topic, or flow into next line

- enjambement — run-on from the end of one line to beginning of next, creating fluency

If you keep these sound patterns at the back of your mind, you will be able to comment on them in the course of your exam answer as another aspect of the text(s) you are analysing.

Delivery and performance of texts

Commenting on delivery is particularly relevant to Question 1, as the focus of this question is entirely on dramatic texts intended for performance. Nevertheless, you are asked to respond to a *written* version of this 'performable' text, and in the exam you can only *imagine* how the passage might sound in performance — what emphasis an actor might place on a word, the pitch and volume of his or her voice, the overall pace etc. You may, of course, have seen a live production in the theatre or on film, and will have your own recollections of the delivery of certain characters or speeches.

It is wise to keep comments on performance relatively brief. Referring to what an actor did in a performance you saw can be helpful (even if you disagreed with the interpretation) because it shows your alertness to performance effects. However, if you have not seen a play 'live', don't indulge in speculation.

Genre and generic structure

Talk in plays

The term 'dramatic discourse' is a kind of linguistic shorthand for 'language used in plays'. Paul Simpson (1997) suggests that that there are two communicative layers at work in dramatic discourse:
- interaction within the play (character-to-character dialogue)
- communication outside the play (between the dramatist and audience or reader)

If you remember that this 'dual communicative structure' exists in every piece of dramatic dialogue, it should help you to analyse any dramatic text you encounter in the exam. Simpson proposes the following useful checklist (though not every point will necessarily be relevant to your exam text).

Discourse structure
- Are the exchange structures symmetrical (i.e. opening moves followed by supporting moves)? If not, does one character disrupt the framework of exchanges? Is this part of his/her characterisation?
- Which character initiates the exchanges and which character responds? What do you learn about each character from this?
- How long are each speaker's turns? Who talks the most, and why?

- Does any character interrupt another? What deductions can be made about these characters?

Discourse strategies

Conversational maxims (including relevance)

- Are Grice's conversational maxims supported or flouted?
- Are there many implied meanings (implicatures)? If so, are they linked with character?
- Is the dialogue easy to follow and relevant? If not, why has the dramatist made it less accessible?

Politeness phenomena

- Are characters differentiated by use of politeness strategies?
- Are there differences in status, power or social distance between characters? How are these shown?
- Is there a balance between face-threatening and face-supportive speech acts?

When you analyse a drama text, if you remember that it is a crafted text intended to reveal character, further the plot or narrative and create mood and atmosphere (via Simpson's 'dual communicative structure'), you won't go far wrong.

Talk in poetry

Talk in poetry is even more structured than in drama, because the poetic form (e.g. ballad, sonnet, ode, dramatic monologue) imposes its own structure and expectations. Even more structure is added by the inevitable imposition of metre, rhyme and rhythm. Thus, speech or dialogue in poetry has a built-in straitjacket — only the poet is able to unbuckle the jacket and create fluent, natural-sounding speech in dialogue or monologue. There are several strategies that the poet can use to achieve this:

- using the poetic voice or persona as a vehicle of expression
- using a narrative voice representing the character who speaks
- using reported or direct speech as part of the poem's structure
- using a mixture of the above

The role of the poet is similar to that of the dramatist — he or she may also wish to create character (and, in a narrative poem, to further the plot). The poet needs to create mood and atmosphere, and perhaps above all to express and evoke emotion. When you look at conversations or monologues in poetry, you must be aware of all this before looking for discourse patterns and strategies. They will be there, but in more modified and less obvious ways.

A poet may use the simple strategy of switching between narrative voices as a way of recreating talk evocatively. For example, the poets Robert Frost and Robert Browning use a single narrative voice to reveal their speaker's character and emotions through crafted monologic speech ('Out, Out!', 'A Servant to Servants', 'My Last

Duchess'). Conversation or dialogue within a poem can also be a way of conveying character, plot, atmosphere and emotion — you can therefore apply discourse analysis to it.

The most important point to remember is that in such a tightly organised literary genre as poetry, talk features will be present only selectively — there will be something interesting to talk about (otherwise the text would not have been deemed suitable for the exam paper) but don't expect the full range encountered in dramatic discourse. Of course, phonology and sound patterning will be important to analyse, as will figurative language; both relate not only to the speaker(s) but also to the meaning of the poem as a whole.

Talk in fiction

Prose fiction makes use of talk in different contexts as part of its narrative structure:
- in direct conversations between characters, major or minor
- in reported or indirect speech
- in free indirect style (first-person experience is communicated through third-person voice: when, in *Pride and Prejudice*, Elizabeth Bennett hears some cruel gossip, Austen writes: 'Elizabeth was shocked to think that, however incapable of such coarseness of expression herself, the coarseness of the sentiment was little other than her own breast had formerly harboured and fancied liberal!')
- through the point of view of one, several or many characters
- through the voice of an omniscient narrator
- through stream-of-consciousness technique, where a character's thoughts are written as randomly as they occur in the mind (e.g. Molly Bloom's soliloquy in *Ulysses* or the eponymous heroine in Virginia Woolf's *Mrs Dalloway*)

Because writers of fiction have the opportunity to be much more expansive in their writing than poets or dramatists, one novel may include many varieties of *crafted* talk, used in whatever context or situation the writer chooses. Be prepared for a whole range of different strategies, and also be aware that 'the talk' will almost certainly be part of plot-based narrative, and may well be framed by extensive description of place or atmosphere. Your focus in Question 2 will be on the dialogue — and there should be plenty to comment on (particularly if it is a realist novel) regarding the usual artistic purposes of revealing character, furthering the plot and describing situation and mood.

Addressing Question 1

Studying the language of pre-1770 texts

The plays set for Question 1 may be written by any dramatist from 1590 to 1770 — just under 200 years of theatre. This period covers the development of the English language from early modern to modern, and all the plays can be demanding to read. So far, most of the set texts have been by Shakespeare, with Wycherley and Sheridan as recent additions. Many of you have encountered Shakespeare before, but not necessarily in great detail, and you may be even less familiar with the other dramatists.

As Question 1 requires you to explain the dialogue in detail from the perspective of discourse and conversation analysis, you need to be confident that you have a good understanding of the play as a whole, and of the way individual dramatic effects are achieved. The purpose of this section is not only to help you feel more confident about analysing early texts, but also to suggest ways of understanding them better and writing about them more effectively. Shakespeare is used as the exemplar dramatist in this section, but there are some references to Restoration and eighteenth-century playwrights.

The contemporary context

When a twenty-first-century audience watches a production of a Shakespeare play, its members have a reasonable awareness (often acquired in primary school) of what the Elizabethan theatre looked like some 400 years ago. The recent success of the film *Shakespeare in Love* has improved this understanding. We know that the rich watched from the stage itself or from boxes, while the poor and 'lowlife' squashed together in the pit. Most people know also that boys played women's roles (with the attendant problems for the actors) and that the original texts still in existence today are often prompt copies.

A significant change in acting style took place in the late sixteenth- and early seventeenth-century theatre — from a 'full-on' rhetorical style to a 'personation' (the creation of individual characters). Political events outside the theatre would then — as now — be alluded to or recognised wryly by the audience (a classical example is the issue of succession in history plays set safely in the fifteenth century, such as Shakespeare's *Richard III* or *Henry IV*).

The Elizabethan or Jacobean dramatist, just like the modern playwright, sought to delight, entertain, shock and disturb the audience through the creation of interesting characters, exciting plots, powerful language and dramatic effects. Your task is to study these early plays and as far as possible show how they work in performance and achieve maximum impact on an audience. You will need to be imaginative and combine your understanding of theatre four centuries ago with your response to contemporary reading and performance of these plays.

Studying seventeenth- and eighteenth-century plays is less arduous for a modern reader. Although the political and social events of this period may seem nearly as far off as Elizabethan England, the language of these later playwrights is more accessible and nearer to modern English, and prose tends to be the chosen medium. Restoration theatre was different from Jacobean theatre in other ways, although many respectable citizens still avoided it. Women were now permitted to act on stage and even took 'breeches parts' where they cross-dressed — much to the delight of the audience. Plays tended to satirise contemporary society and moral values.

Getting used to the pentameter

Returning to the sixteenth century, it is often said that **blank verse** (iambic pentameter) is one of the greatest achievements of Elizabethan theatre. Its flexibility and power were exploited not only by John Milton in the seventeenth century but by William Wordsworth in the nineteenth century and even some twentieth-century poets. You may feel that this is an exaggerated view of its importance — we don't talk in blank verse today, so why is it so great?

Blank verse has five beats to a line, but the performer or playwright *can* add an extra beat to enhance the meaning without losing the underlying harmony and rhythm. For example, in the following extract from *Hamlet*, most actors will play around with the conventional beats (marked in bold) according to their own interpretation of the tortured prince's character:

> To **be**, or **not** to **be** — that **is** the **ques**tion;
> **Whether** 'tis **nobler in** the **mind** to **suffer**
> The **slings** and **arrows of** out**rage**ous **fort**une
> Or **to** take **arms against** a **sea** of **troubles**
> And **by** opposing, **end** them.

Hamlet III.i.56–60

As you read blank verse, keep this amazing flexibility in mind; it can come very close to sounding like 'real' speech. The contemporary American dramatist David Mamet, writing in the *Guardian*, argues that 'the dramatic line should be written to convince primarily through its rhyme and rhythm and only secondarily, if at all, through an appeal to reason'. This point is supported vigorously by another contemporary dramatist, Glyn Maxwell, who defends iambic pentameter passionately as the 'natural medium for the stage', arguing that it allows actors to use breath to create human sound ('all the wit and learning in the world can't compensate for an inability to render persuasively the distinct voice of an actual breathing person').

For Maxwell, 'the greatest tool in the service of this art is the line of five beats, the pentameter...no more nor less natural in the day of Shakespeare than it is today. It simply seems to hold as an approximation of the breath, and as such, serves as a metaphor for the experience of a moment. Neither verse nor prose has found a better one.' Such views from contemporary theatre practitioners offer impressive support for a 400-year-old verse form.

When you read blank verse, tune your inner ear to the sound of the five beats, and the 'breath' behind it. These factors work to enhance the dramatist's, the character's and the actor's communication of meaning.

So what about prose?

Shakespeare used prose differently across his creative span. The proportion of prose to poetry is variable up to 1600, after which the ratio is 80% poetry, 20% prose. Genre is a significant factor: history and tragedy tend to use more poetry than prose (with exceptions such as the character of Falstaff in *Henry IV*), whereas comedy (*Much Ado About Nothing*, *As You Like It* and *Twelfth Night*) contains a high proportion of prose. Characters of lower social status often speak in prose, such as Bottom and his friends in *A Midsummer Night's Dream* or the drunken porter in *Macbeth*. On the other hand, prose is used by Hamlet, Prince of Denmark, as well as by characters such as Beatrice and Benedick from *Much Ado About Nothing*, and by Sir Toby, Sir Andrew and the socially aspiring Malvolio in *Twelfth Night*.

When you meet prose in a Shakespeare extract, you should decide on whether it is meant to communicate 'low' comedy, whether it represents the sophisticated repartee of the court, or whether it is used to convey complex messages about character in a tragedy such as *Hamlet*. Look for the 'best fit' and for other clues, such as register, lexical choice and absence or presence of humour.

Prose in seventeenth- and eighteenth-century plays, however, functions as the natural vehicle for the comedy of manners — its flexibility means that dramatists can switch register from high to low life easily. Occasionally, a romantic scene will be in verse, but this is infrequent.

Pronouns at work

The grammatical roles of pronouns include substitution (e.g. to avoid repetition of someone's name) and emphasis (e.g. to point out something). In a play where the dialogue requires the audience to recognise individuals, personal pronouns are highly significant. First-person singular and plural pronouns (*I*, *me*, *we*, *us*) indicate personal involvement of the speaker, and in the plural form can signify royal status. Second-person pronouns are interesting because the familiar '*thee*' and '*thou*' forms were used freely in sixteenth- and seventeenth-century English between *social equals* (whether upper- or lower-class) or by upper-class speakers addressing a social inferior. The polite '*you*' was used by everyone when addressing a social superior or someone unfamilar. Interestingly, God, animals and things were also addressed as '*thou*'.

This is important for you to understand because if you comment on pronoun usage in an extract, and muddle the '*thou*'/'*you*' difference, it can distort your answer. Remember that social equals could use both '*you*' and '*thou*' to each other — but this might indicate some awareness of 'felt' status difference. This practice remained the same through the sixteenth and seventeenth centuries, but by the eighteenth century, '*you*' became closer to the norm.

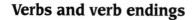

Verbs and verb endings

Verbs are always worth examining closely, because of what they tell us about the representation of time and action in a text. Verb endings can confuse an inexperienced reader of sixteenth- and seventeenth-century English, because the suffixes '-*est*' and '-*th*' have disappeared from modern standard English. Significantly, these suffixes were second- and third-person singular forms linked with the singular pronouns '*thou*', '*he*', '*she*' and '*it*', and the conjugation was '*I do*', '*thou doest*' and '*he doth*'. These pronoun and verb forms are archaisms today — but you need to be aware that they were normal usage when the set play was written.

The problem of archaism

The concept of archaism is worth knowing about when you are studying pre-1770 texts, and there is a scale of degree of obscurity. Words which are completely unfamiliar and/or relate to outdated social practices are described as **archaic** or **obsolete**. However, words which have changed their meaning in some way but which you half understand can be described as **partially obsolete** or **outdated**. Words which you recognise and apply to social practices you have heard about, but which no longer happen, can be described as **old-fashioned** or **outdated**. In other words, don't use the term **archaism** unless it is an accurate description (in other words a pre-eighteenth-century word).

Unfortunately, the only way to deal with completely unfamiliar words is to make sure you have looked them up long before the examination. Don't just guess the meaning — you might get it horribly wrong and entertain the examiner in a way you hadn't intended. Check out all doubtful words and phrases for yourself, as part of your detailed preparation of the play — this is your responsibility, not your teacher's.

The play as actor's text

The film *Shakespeare in Love* provides a convincingly imagined insight into the intensely pressured world of Elizabethan theatre, where plays were written at high speed, and theatre companies depended upon patronage (preferably royal) and public interest to succeed. Actors and writers worked together closely, and parts were often written to suit individual actors (such as Will Kemp). As a result, the text of any one play might consist simply of actors' scripts plus the theatrical prompt book. It is not surprising that this led, after Shakespeare's death, to significant problems for editors when establishing their final 'approved' version. In contrast, the texts of Restoration and eighteenth-century plays are unproblematic.

Shakespeare and his editors

Establishing the text

No one is really sure of how Heminge and Condell, Shakespeare's first editors, did in fact establish the text of each play. As we saw above, many people had a hand in it.

Based on several corrected versions, a copy was submitted to the Master of the Revels for official licensing. Even this version might have been changed later. According to Heminge and Condell, who produced the First Folio, there were many 'stolen and surreptitious copies, maimed and deformed by the frauds and stealths of injurious imposters'. This is hardly surprising!

What is important for you to recognise is that *no one really knows today* exactly what Shakespeare's intentions were. You can make reasoned judgements, based on context and characterisation. Indeed, your thoughtful interpretation of a line or passage, argued clearly and supported by textual reference, could provide a valuable new insight into one of Shakespeare's plays.

The problem of punctuation

It should now be clear that basing an argument in Question 1 on *'Shakespeare's punctuation'* is not valid. Decisions about punctuating his plays have been made over the centuries by his editors, not by Shakespeare, as they do their best to make sense of the 'maimed and deformed' texts.

By all means, comment on the dramatic effect produced by an exclamation or a question as an interesting *grammatical* feature. Avoid, however, suggesting that Shakespeare intends to make a specific effect by 'his punctuation'.

Actors, directors and other interpretations

The final bullet point in Question 1 refers to 'delivery of lines in performance'. This is intended to give you an opportunity to refer to any relevant theatre or film production of your set play that you have seen. It is *not* a general invitation to *speculate* on how you think the play should be directed. Candidates who have not seen a production may briefly suggest an interpretation or performance option of a set passage — any more is inappropriate.

- Don't generalise about the production you saw — commenting specifically on how the set passages were delivered will help your argument.
- Don't launch into an extensive discussion of how you believe the scene or passage could have been performed better.
- Remember that any reference to performance must support your overall analysis and not act as a piece of separate theatre criticism.

Achieving dramatic effects

The term **dramatic effects** refers simply to the way in which the dramatist and audience act and react in relation to each other. The writer uses all of his or her creative resources (especially language) to engage the audience's emotional and intellectual response to the performance of the play. Your task in this examination is to explore in detail how this engagement is achieved in your particular set passages, with a major focus being the crafting of speech into dialogue.

The rubric for Question 1 (see p. 8) states that candidates should:

Discuss the ways in which the **two** passages reveal the playwright's skills in producing **specific dramatic effects**.

The following paragraphs focus on what this means and how dramatic effects are created, looking at each bullet point separately.

Context

The importance of knowing the context *before* and *after* the set extracts cannot be overstated. You must know the play backwards and inside out — not easy, but necessary.

- With this level of detailed knowledge, you will be alert to the effect achieved by **dramatic and situational irony**, creating a relationship with the audience. For example, the audience becomes increasingly aware of Othello's blindness to Iago's manipulation every time the word 'honest' is used.
- Another effect linked directly with context is the **revelation of character** through plot, action, interaction or soliloquy. A classic example is the way the audience learns about Hamlet's state of mind as his soliloquies develop. Another example would be as we watch Malvolio's arrogant behaviour and understand the plotters' desire to see his downfall.
- The choice of **register**, **idiolect** and **vocabulary** can also be linked with the context of the extract.
- It is also possible to make relevant reference to **theories of power relations** and **gender relations** in connection with context.

Spoken language features and discourse conventions

You need a thorough understanding of spoken language features, discourse conventions and non-fluency features in order to be able to identify effects achieved by the dramatist. In every case you will have to *identify* a feature or pattern of speech and *explain* how it works to create a particular effect. For example, the dramatist has crafted dialogue to fit the idiolect of individual characters, progress the plot, reveal character and relationships between characters, by showing the way they interact with each other. You may find it useful to refer to some linguistic theories here (where relevant), especially those relating to *politeness strategies, successful and unsuccessful conversation, power relations* and *gender relations*.

Literary, grammatical and rhetorical devices

We have already discussed earlier how literary, grammatical and rhetorical devices can be used to create particular effects.

Example of a literary device in *Othello*

Othello, intent on killing the innocently sleeping Desdemona, gazes at her 'whiter skin than snow/And smooth as monumental alabaster' (V.ii.4–5). The **similes** are particularly powerful, since alabaster is associated with the cold beauty of carved figures on tombs, and Desdemona is about to die. The dramatic effect of this literary device on the audience, which is aware of Othello's terrible error, is an extremely powerful one.

Example of a grammatical device in *A Midsummer Night's Dream*

Hermia's anger with Helena and Lysander is expressed through the grammatical device of **questions** and **exclamations**: 'And are you grown so high in his esteem/Because I am so dwarfish and so low?/How low am I, thou painted maypole? Speak!/How low am I?'(III.ii.294–97). The repetition of **interrogatives**, together with the visual humour of the tall and short girls, creates a strongly comic effect.

Example of a rhetorical device in *Hamlet*

Hamlet, grieving at his father's death and mother's marriage, uses the rhetorical devices of **listing** and **incrementum** to express his pain: 'How weary, stale, flat, and unprofitable/Seem to me all the uses of this world!' (I.ii.133–34). The effect on the audience is highly emotive, as it conveys Hamlet's suicidal mood.

Phonological features

These features are a kind of 'mixed bag' — you can comment on dramatic effects produced by everything phonological from rhyme and rhythm to puns and poetic devices such as assonance and alliteration. Add to this the effects of the actor's delivery of lines, variation in pace, volume, pitch and tone, and you have plenty of scope for comment. The passage from *Hamlet* shown below comes from the First Player's speech (II.ii.469–72) when he is showing off his acting skills to Hamlet. It describes the Greek hero Pyrrhus attacking the Trojan king Priam:

> Unequal matched,
> **P**yrrhus at **Pri**am drives, in rage strikes wide,
> But with the **whiff** and **w**ind of his fell sword
> Th' unnerved **f**ather **f**alls.

The combination of alliteration, assonance and a high proportion of single-syllable words creates the effect of blow after blow being struck. This would probably be enhanced by the actor's exaggerated delivery.

Other relevant aspects

You can also comment on any other feature of note in either of the two passages that does not fit under the other headings in this section. For example, a *brief* reference to staging or costume might be made, supporting a point made earlier in your answer, or you might make a *short* comment about a significant social or political issue (such as Elizabeth's potential successor or the rise of Puritanism) as a factor affecting audience response. If you have a *brief* but illuminating addition to make to your discussion, this is where you could fit it in.

Planning an answer to Question 1

The outline below is only a suggestion — it is descriptive, not prescriptive. However, it may help you to see the way your answer should be structured and illustrated.

Opening paragraph

You should contextualise each passage briefly in relation to the immediate situation (the event or scene before and after) and position in relation to the play as a whole. Comment on what is happening to the key characters in each passage, and how this is likely to affect the audience. In other words, what are the dramatist's aims and purposes in each passage?

Second paragraph

You may find it helpful to follow the structure established in the previous section on dramatic effect. In this case, the second paragraph would focus on context in more detail, after you have identified and explained the balance between verse and prose. What is the overall tone or mood of the passage? What will the audience discover in terms of theme, character, relationships and plot?

Third, fourth and/or fifth paragraphs

In these paragraphs (and in no particular order) you should discuss *sound patterning* and *phonological features*, *interactional features* and *lexico-grammatical features*. You should show how they help to create specific dramatic effects and provide textual support.

Concluding paragraph

This will probably be brief, and may refer to both passages together. At this stage you may find it useful to make one or two comparisons between the passages in relation to language choice or treatment of overall themes — but *only* if you have time.

Hints and tips

Successful candidates:
- know their set play back to front and inside out, including what happens in each scene and act; it is *not* enough to 'know the story'
- *always* bear in mind how the audience would respond to whatever literary or linguistic device is being used
- are able to identify and explain interesting literary and linguistic features without working to an obvious mental checklist

Less successful candidates:
- fail to check the exact wording of the question

- get the context wrong and/or spend too long talking about the play as a whole because they don't know where the set passage comes from
- talk about dramatic effects in general terms but with no textual support
- even worse — they don't mention dramatic effects

Addressing Question 2

Making sense of transcripts

In Question 2 you will be given two passages of transcribed conversation, paired with two literary passages, to choose from. Some candidates find it difficult to read transcribed speech, so this section will look at the process of transcription in more detail.

Although all transcribers want to record what is said in a given exchange, the complexity and detail of transcription vary. Some variations of transcription are listed below, in order of increasing complexity. (The kind of transcript which includes complex phonetic detail has been omitted as it is not relevant to this examination.)

- The transcript simply records the utterances of each speaker (occasionally — and misleadingly — using punctuation, which is applicable only to *written* language).
- The transcript includes pauses, fillers, hesitations and self-repairs (normal non-fluency features).
- The transcript includes discourse features such as interruptions, overlappings and latched speech.

If it is necessary to indicate pitch, volume or intonation on a transcript, this will be glossed carefully. It is unlikely that the transcribed passages in your examination will include any features other than those described above. Furthermore, a key will always be provided explaining the symbols used in each transcribed passage. (This is not an English Language specification and you are not required to understand phonetic symbols.) A basic key follows:

(.)	pause or micropause
(0.5)	pause (in fractions of minute)
...	pause
=	latching (following on directly from previous speaker)
[ ]	overlap with other speakers

Getting comfortable with transcripts

To make the best of Question 2 you need to be a confident transcript reader, so you are not 'thrown' by different situations where spoken exchanges take place, or by an unfamiliar transcription symbol. It is important to experience as much transcribed speech as possible, from casual conversation to service encounters, business and professional interviews, and unscripted radio and television exchanges. It is also important to practise reading 'unseen' transcripts within a time-constrained situation. You will be presented with unseen extracts in the examination, and you need to be comfortable reading them at speed without missing details. The seven transcribed extracts below present you with some opportunities to identify for yourself genre, context, situation, purposes and likely audience.

Example 1

GERMAINE GREER:	hello and welcome to the last in the present series of *The Last Word* (.) what we've been trying to do is to civilise the talk-show by avoiding slanging matches and looking for consensus (.) we're also interested in giving an insight into how women think

Example 2

MOTORIST:	go straight ahead for a mile =
PEDESTRIAN:	= yes =
MOTORIST:	ignore the left fork
PEDESTRIAN:	ignore the left fork
MOTORIST:	yeah (.) then I get to some traffic lights =
PEDESTRIAN:	= you get to some traffic lights (.) turn right at the traffic lights (.) carry
MOTORIST:	huhhuh
PEDESTRIAN:	on down there that's the main road into York

Example 3

TEACHER:	a glowing splint tests for (2.5) not hydrogen even (3.0) not hydrogen even (.) no (.)
PUPIL 1:	oxygen
TEACHER:	oxygen (0.5) what does it do to it Nichola
PUPIL 2:	relights the splint

TEACHER:	relights the splint (0.5) what's the test for hydrogen then since that one's been brought up (.) Andrea
PUPIL 3:	I don't know
TEACHER:	it's something to do with a splint (1.0) have a go (3.0) no (.) Zoe

Example 4

CHRIS EVANS:	so erm you're...you're very...erm...you're very successful on the girl front aren't you generally
JAMIE THEAKSTON:	*[coughs slightly]* what do you mean by that *[audience laughs]*
CHRIS EVANS:	well I mean you're very successful with...erm girls you do tend to have a lot of beautiful girlfriends
JAMIE THEAKSTON:	er...I don't know exactly what you mean I...I have a girlfriend
CHRIS EVANS:	you have a girlfriend now
JAMIE THEAKSTON:	yeah
CHRIS EVANS:	but you...you...you do you are very successful in that field *[Jamie laughs]*

Example 5

PATIENT:	...yesterday I got home from work and [inaudible] the trouble is I can't bend forward and I can't turn like sideways it's like the bottom of my spine it just feels like I'm sitting on a pin
DOCTOR:	so it's pain in the lower back
PATIENT:	lower back just about there
DOCTOR:	ok how long did you say again
PATIENT:	I mean all last night I couldn't turn on my side I couldn't stand up I couldn't go to the toilet
DOCTOR:	so it got worse overnight
PATIENT:	yeh when I walk it hurts me to walk (.) I don't know what it I don't know if probably it's lifting the residents in the nursing home or what

Example 6

YOUNG FEMALE:	are we getting close to Adelaide yet
OLDER FEMALE:	yes
YOUNG FEMALE:	uhuh
OLDER FEMALE:	are you an American
YOUNG FEMALE:	no I'm Finnish
OLDER FEMALE:	Finnish are you touring this country
YOUNG FEMALE:	yeah well…erm I'm studying for one year here
OLDER FEMALE:	oh are you
YOUNG FEMALE:	yes
OLDER FEMALE:	oh how nice
YOUNG FEMALE:	[laughter] and now
OLDER FEMALE:	and then returning to Finland are you
YOUNG FEMALE:	yes

Example 7

RADIO COMMENTATOR:	here's Burton (.) on the ball for the first time (.) good pass up into the box Darryl Powell there (.) goes to the by-line forces it back [voice rises] but cover is good (.) it is Charret and he knocks it away for Derby County's fourth corner (..) fifth corner (..) fifth corner of the game (.) all in the second half actually (..) Schoor is going to take the corner (.) Derby trail two–nil (..) here it comes (.) from the left-hand side not good enough (.) it's headed out by Rod Lee (.) big chase back for Darryl Powell (.) nearly back to the half-way line (.) he gets it played it to Prior (..) Prior is tackled very late [voice rises] that's free-kick and it might be a booking actually as well (..) yes

Characterising spontaneous or unplanned texts

The transcribed extracts in the previous section represent different kinds of spontaneous speech in a variety of contexts. Just to consider them as *visual representations of speech* confirms powerfully that generic difference does exist in spoken language and its transcribed versions. For example, look at the obvious visual contrast between the dense continuous text of example 7 and the short, almost monosyllabic exchange in example 6.

As you read through a wide variety of transcripts for practice (and the transcribed extracts in your examination), remember that there are four elements to focus on:

- speakers
- context
- audience
- purposes

For example, in examples 1 and 7, although there is only one speaker in each extract, internal evidence in both suggests that Germaine Greer is introducing a broadcast discussion with other people, and that the radio commentator will be sharing the football commentary with another colleague. Both conclusions are based on our previous knowledge of the frame and schema of the two genres, broadcast talk-show and sports commentary.

Similarly, in examples 3 and 5, we recognise the familiar teacher–pupil and doctor–patient situations, or schemas, and are able to deduce the likely contexts (classroom, consulting room), and the differing purposes (to elicit and confirm knowledge, to gain information in order to make a diagnosis).

The purposes in examples 2 and 6 are rather different: in example 2 the motorist is looking for directions and seeking information; in example 6 although there is some information seeking, the exchange is primarily phatic as the two women travellers establish friendly relations on their shared train journey.

You are the only person who can improve your transcript reading and interpreting skills through lots of practice. If you ever get really stuck with a transcribed passage, try a little *empathy* — imagine yourself in the situation of the speakers, and this should help you to understand what is going on in the exchange. Making your own transcripts (however short) of as many different kinds of talk as possible is the best way of 'getting comfortable' with transcribed speech.

Top tips with transcripts

- Identify context and situation.
- Identify possible schema and structures of expectation.
- Identify speakers and purposes.
- Identify audience (even monologues are addressing the self).
- Note the effect of audience on speakers' lexical and grammatical choices.
- Note the effect of audience on speakers' discourse patterns.
- Empathise with speakers in context and situation.

Characterising crafted texts

The crafted or literary texts used in this part of the examination have several clearly recognisable and important characteristics. First, they each represent a specific literary genre or sub-genre. Second, the purpose of any literary text is whatever the author intends. Third, they have something in common with the transcribed extract. The link with the transcribed text may be a shared genre or topic, a similar context or situation, or a common purpose. It is usually not too difficult to recognise a link — but more about link-seeking later in this section.

The literary genres from which an examination passage might be taken range from prose fiction (novels, romances, short stories, detective stories etc.) to poetry (sonnet, lyric, narrative poem, ballad etc.) and modern drama (including comedy, tragedy, comedy of manners etc.). You need to be able to recognise these genres. In the examination, a choice between two of the three major genres will be available. Don't assume you can second-guess the June paper genre options on the basis of the previous January's paper — there is no official requirement to vary the literary genres between each session.

An area which can cause problems for candidates is the question of authorial *purpose* in crafted texts. The chief difficulty is that candidates forget that the literary text is crafted by an author, and it is the author alone whose purpose it is to create the characters, invent their conversations and describe the situation, mood or action during which the crafted conversation takes place.

For example, in a past paper candidates were asked to compare the recent transcript of a casual conversation between two female students over a sandwich with the scene in Jane Austen's novel *Pride and Prejudice,* where the two older Bennett sisters, who have been away from home, have lunch with their younger sisters and are told about the latest gossip. Austen's purpose in the passage is to reveal *character* (i.e. to show the folly of Lydia and Kitty, and the embarrassment and annoyance felt by Elizabeth and Jane). Other purposes are to *further the plot* by letting the audience know new information (the regiment is leaving for Brighton) and to *amuse* the audience through the use of irony in her descriptions of the private room at the inn, the dismissing of the waiter, Lydia's hat purchase and the squashed journey home.

The purposes of the characters *within* the crafted text may also be relevant, but they are still manipulated by the author. The 'purposes' of the characters are relatively simple in the passage described above: the younger sisters wish to give information and the older sisters wish to listen without revealing their real feelings. Again, these character-led purposes are created by Austen to give the reader further insights.

In the literary genres of poetry and drama, the literary purposes of the poet or dramatist may be different from those of the novelist. For example, poetry, with its sharp, structured focus may be more directly *expressive* of heightened thought and emotion than fiction, which offers more expansive space and time. The poet can *describe* a scene or a character as vividly as a novelist, but has to be more selective in choosing the evocative detail. The dramatist, on the other hand, has no need to *describe* a scene if the staging creates a representation of reality. For the dramatist, dialogue is the medium on which the creation of character and plot depend, conveyed through the action. As in prose fiction, broader themes and connecting threads in plays may emerge only gradually.

To summarise: all literary texts share the authorial purposes of crafting plot, creating character, expressing emotion, describing scenes and mood — but in different proportions, depending on the genre.

Finally, *make sure that you read all the information given in the question* about the crafted literary texts. This information is intended to help you make sense of the passages more quickly as they are unseen. It does not impress examiners when a candidate throws marks away unnecessarily by getting a matter of simple fact wrong (thus spoiling his/her argument), when the correct information was there all the time in the rubric.

Making effective comparisons

The most important instruction in Question 2 is to *compare* the texts. Whichever option you choose, your first task must be to decide what the passages have in common. The main difference between the texts, of course, is the fact that one is spontaneous speech and the other is carefully crafted literary dialogue. Always bearing this central difference in mind, you may find the checklist below helpful in developing your comparison.

- Start by identifying the literary genre.
- Is the *situation* or *context* similar in each text? (e.g. someone lost is asking for directions; two strangers conversing on a train; mother and children talking)
- Is the *frame* or *schema* similar? (e.g. an interview; a medical consultation; service encounter)
- Is the *format* similar? (e.g. is there only one speaker in each text, or are several speakers involved?)
- Is the *purpose* of the speakers similar? (e.g. to exchange information/gossip; to give information, describe and evaluate action, as in a sports commentary; to exchange information, express attitudes and persuade, as in business negotiations)
- What can we learn about the speaker's character (values) and attitudes (feelings) from what he/she says or does, or from how he/she is described by the author or other participants in the exchange?

You should find this checklist links usefully with the bullet points provided in the question. These should always be used as a basis for your comparison of the two texts. The first bullet point is likely to focus on context, situation or schema; the second will probably be concerned with functions or purposes; the third and/or fourth will definitely be linked with the expression of attitudes and values, but may also be linked with structure and point of view.

Your comparison of the texts should use these broad headings, but must be focused *not* generalised; you are expected to provide detailed linguistic and/or literary evidence to support your points of comparison between the spontaneous and crafted texts.

Planning an answer to Question 2

Because the unseen texts in Question 2a are completely different from those in Question 2b, you should note that:
- There will be completely different information in the rubric about each pair of texts.
- The bullet points for each question may be different.
- Both questions require you to *compare* the spontaneous transcript with the literary extract.

The outline described below can be applied to either Question 2a or 2b. It is only a suggested outline and is in no way prescriptive.

Opening paragraph

Start by identifying the *common* context, theme, purpose or genre between the texts (see above). You may want to make clear that you are aware of the basic differences between spontaneous and crafted speech. This is useful, not just because it gives the examiner confidence in your answer, but because it provides *you* with a quick summary and mental checklist.

Note any obvious *differences* such as audience and/or purpose. It is important to establish clearly in this opening paragraph that you are making a comparison.

Second paragraph

Focus on comparing context and situation here, and on how this is revealed by similarities and differences in lexical and grammatical choice, discourse features, register, spoken language features, sound patterning etc. Ensure you show clear awareness of the central role of the participants in the transcribed exchange, and the role of the author in *crafting* the literary text.

Third paragraph

This paragraph is likely to be linked with differences in purpose and function — but not necessarily. Be prepared to adjust your comparison according to the exact wording of the bullet point in the question; make sure you choose relevant textual detail to support your argument.

Fourth paragraph

This bullet point is usually linked with how *attitudes* and *values* are expressed or conveyed by the speakers in the transcribed exchange, and are communicated by the author in the literary text. To get this right (and many candidates find this particular bullet point difficult) you need to look for lexis or grammar or discourse features which relate to *emotion*, express *opinion*, are *evaluative* or reflect moral or ethical *values*.

Fifth paragraph and/or conclusion

This bullet point may invite you to comment on any other aspects you think are relevant — or you can move straight into the conclusion, where you look at the comparative analysis and note any particularly interesting differences or similarities between talk in real life and talk in literature.

Hints and tips

Successful candidates:
- read the information about each text in the rubric carefully to ensure they have a clear understanding of who is talking, to whom and for what purpose
- check that they have recognised the literary genre and/or the schema in the transcript
- make sure they compare the texts throughout their answer
- give detailed textual support to their arguments

Less successful candidates:
- don't read the information about each text
- are unaware of the differences between spontaneous and crafted talk, and write about them as if they were identical
- describe the texts rather than analyse them
- forget to provide any detailed evidence from the texts
- focus on content of conversational exchanges rather than on how they function
- forget to compare the texts

Questions
&
Answers

This section is intended to give you the chance to see how A- and C-grade candidates have answered a range of questions on **Unit 5: Talk in Life and Literature**.

The first part focuses on Question 1, with an example of an A- and a C-grade answer as well as two exemplar commentaries. The second part focuses on Question 2, and again provides an example of an A- and a C-grade answer, and one exemplar commentary.

Throughout this section, candidates' answers are accompanied by examiner comments, preceded by the icon *e*.

Question 1: English drama pre-1770

Read the *two* passages from the play you have studied.

Discuss the ways in which these two passages reveal the playwright's skills in producing *specific dramatic effects*.

In your answer you should consider:
- context (including brief reference to the play as a whole)
- spoken language features and discourse conventions
- literary, grammatical and rhetorical devices
- phonological features, including delivery of lines in performance
- any other relevant aspects

A Midsummer Night's Dream

Passage A

DEMETRIUS:	I love thee not, therefore pursue me not.
	Where is Lysander, and fair Hermia?
	The one I'll slay; the other slayeth me.
	Thou toldest me they were stolen unto this wood,
	And here I am, and wood within this wood
	Because I cannot meet my Hermia.
	Hence, get thee gone, and follow me no more!
HELENA:	You draw me, you hard-hearted adamant!
	But yet you draw not iron: for my heart
	Is true as steel. Leave you your power to draw,
	And I shall have no power to follow you.
DEMETRIUS:	Do I entice you? Do I speak you fair?
	Or rather do I not in plainest truth
	Tell you I do not nor I cannot love you?
HELENA:	And even for that do I love you the more.
	I am your spaniel; and, Demetrius,
	The more you beat me I will fawn on you.
	Use me but as your spaniel: spurn me, strike me,

question

Neglect me, lose me; only give me leave,
Unworthy as I am, to follow you.
What worser place can I beg in your love —
And yet a place of high respect with me —
Than to be usèd as you use your dog?

DEMETRIUS: Tempt not too much the hatred of my spirit;
For I am sick when I do look on thee.

HELENA: And I am sick when I look not on you.

Passage B

MUSTARDSEED: What's your will?

BOTTOM: Nothing, good Monsieur, but to help Cavalery Cobweb to scratch. I must to the barber's, Monsieur, for methinks I am marvellous hairy about the face. And I am such a tender ass, if my hair do but tickle me, I must scratch.

TITANIA: What, wilt thou hear some music, my sweet love?

BOTTOM: I have a reasonable good ear in music. Let's have the tongs and the bones.

TITANIA: Or say, sweet love, what thou desirest to eat.

BOTTOM: Truly, a peck of provender. I could munch your good dry oats. Methinks I have a great desire to a bottle of hay. Good hay, sweet hay hath no fellow.

TITANIA: I have a venturous fairy that shall seek
The squirrel's hoard, and fetch thee new nuts.

BOTTOM: I had rather have a handful or two of dried pease.
But, I pray you, let none of your people stir me:
I have an exposition of sleep come upon me.

TITANIA: Sleep thou, and I will wind thee in my arms.
Faeries be gone, and be all ways away. [*Exeunt Fairies*]
So doth the woodbine the sweet honeysuckle
Gently entwist; the female ivy so
Enrings the barky fingers of the elm.
Oh how I love thee! How I dote on thee!

A-grade answer

In passages A and B, Shakespeare uses different features of language to convey specific dramatic effects. The first passage is part of a conversation between Demetrius and Helena towards the beginning of the play, after Demetrius has followed Lysander and Hermia to the wood upon Helena's instruction. However, since he has not found the two lovers, Demetrius is angry — regarding both that and the fact that Helena has followed him. His anger and thus the dramatic effect of tension is conveyed through the manner in which he addresses her — he uses the impersonal 'thee' as opposed to Helena's personal 'you' in his direction. This in fact could be seen as a break in discourse conventions, although it is not known on whose part this discrepancy would be.

🖉 The candidate addresses the question immediately — and uses the correct word 'convey' as a synonym for 'communicate', not the frequently misused word 'portray'. The candidate could have given more precise context for the passage, i.e. Act II Scene ii, but does provide clear, accurate detail. The comment on the use of 'thee' and 'you' is the wrong way round — 'thee' is the familiar form between social equals or between a social superior and inferior; 'you' is the general polite usage. Nevertheless, the candidate's point about dramatic tension is valid. The final comment in this paragraph is vague and needs more explanation.

Furthermore, Demetrius's frustration with Helena is also conveyed through his interrogatives: 'Do I entice you? Do I speak you fair?' It is clear that he finds the fact — that Helena is following him when it is Hermia that he desires — entirely unfair, and this attitude is conveyed in his terms of address regarding Hermia: 'fair Hermia' and in the possessive pronoun 'my' he uses to refer to her. This attitude creates a further tension, as well as the dramatic effect of humour — the situation, piteous as it may be, is quite funny.

🖉 There are several mistakes in this paragraph: the 'interrogatives' are actually rhetorical, not direct questions; 'terms of reference' would be more accurate; the possessive pronoun 'my' is actually an adjective. However, the candidate has already mentioned two specific examples of dramatic effect, showing a clear focus and sense of direction.

Helena's language also shows the dramatic effect of humour — her use of imagery in 'I am your spaniel' creates amusement, even more so because, although it is an amusing image, it is made all the more laughable by the fact that, if read, her words could seem in earnest. Her use of listing in 'Use me but as your spaniel, strike me, Neglect me, lose me' — the repetition of 'me' and also the alliteration of 's' in 'spurn' and 'strike' makes Helena sound rather desperate, particularly because the sibilant sound of 's' can sound quite plaintive aloud. So, although the audience may be amused by her outburst, they may also feel sorry for her.

🖉 Because the candidate uses the adjective 'sibilant' later in the sentence, it would have been neater to refer to the 'repetition of "s"' rather than introducing the general term 'alliteration'. In this paragraph, the candidate notes how phonological features support figurative language to create a complex emotional effect on the audience — a sophisticated point.

In fact, throughout Helena creates a dramatic effect of sadness through her lexical choices, for example, the exclamative: 'You draw me, you hard-hearted adamant!' This is a break in discourse conventions, as are insults in general, and also a disruption of Grice's maxim of manner. Shakespeare appears to have done this in order to convey the variety of emotions which are tormenting Helena.

> This a short but nicely judged paragraph in which the candidate describes the emotional turmoil affecting Helena — and the audience. Discourse theory is used neatly to show that Helena is not 'speaking in an appropriate manner'. However, the candidate fails to explain the meaning of the image 'adamant'.

When she uses simile in 'But yet you draw not iron: for my heart is true as steel' it is clear from this that she feels very strongly about Demetrius, which would likely also make an audience feel sorry for her. Similarly, in the combination of imperative and declarative 'Leave you your power to draw/And I shall have no power to follow you' Helena's unhappiness at the situation is conveyed, as in her latched talk when answering Demetrius's seemingly rhetorical question 'And even for that do I love you the more'. All of these features are emotive, and designed to make an audience pity Helena.

> There is some confident and accurate use of linguistic terminology here. The candidate continues to be aware of performance and audience response: he/she makes effective use of knowledge of spoken language features when describing the 'run-on' effect of latched talk between Demetrius and Helena.

Similarly, the use of patterning in 'For I am sick when I do look on thee/And I am sick when I look not on you' creates pity for Helena and perhaps dislike for Demetrius, since the pattern of 'sick' in use is rather cruel. Also since the extract is written in iambic pentameter, the patterning in the writing is far more prominent.

> This is potentially a good point, but the candidate has not explained why the extract is in blank verse — because it deals with serious emotion between persons of high status — so the point about patterning needs more back-up.

The second extract is positioned later in the play, after Oberon and Puck have played their trick on Titania — in this extract she is deeply in love with the unfortunate Bottom, who has had his head transfigured into that of an ass — something which appears to have escaped his notice, which causes a large amount of dramatic irony, particularly in the comment: 'And I am such a tender ass if my hair do but tickle me, I must scratch.' The use of the word 'ass' when that is what he has become is intended to be amusing. Furthermore, the comments regarding hay bring further irony, particularly in repetition: 'I have a great desire for a bottle [bundle] of hay. Good hay, sweet hay hath no fellow'. This would be a very strange thing for a human to want to eat, which causes amusement.

🖉 The context of this extract is imprecise (Act IV Scene i) and the scene it comes from could have been explained better. The candidate is aware of the comic aspects of this passage — the dramatic irony of Bottom's words and the general humour of the situation. However, there is no mention of other contexts — exhausted lovers asleep in wood, for example, and the imminence of Titania's rescue by Oberon.

Another aspect of the extract which would be amusing, particularly to an Elizabethan audience, is the obvious class difference between Bottom and Titania: Shakespeare portrays this by writing Titania's sentences in poetry (iambic pentameter) alternated with Bottom's speech in prose. This is intended to show their different classes through the contrasts in sophistication of language.

🖉 This is a good point, but it needs an illustration from the text to clinch it.

Further humour can be found in Titania's terms of address when talking to Bottom 'my sweet love'. This could be seen as a break in discourse conventions, especially since Bottom's lack of sophistication is prominent: when asked if he wished for music, for example, he demands the 'tongs and the bones', which were not particularly good instruments. Also, Bottom can seem quite impolite to Titania when addressing her, especially when his terms of address are compared to hers: 'But I pray you, let none of your people stir me'. It appears as if Bottom is rather enjoying ordering the fairies around, which is unsurprising since later in the play we find out that he believes the encounter with the fairies to be a dream.

🖉 The candidate is aware of the comic contrast between Titania's eloquent, romantic register and Bottom's down-to-earth approach, and makes a brief wider reference to his reaction when he awakes.

When Bottom decides to go to sleep, a further dramatic effect is created — this of amusement mixed with pity. Titania speaks of her love for Bottom, and her infatuation is pitiful, particularly in the anthropomorphising in 'the sweet honeysuckle/Gently entwist; the female ivy so/Enrings the barky fingers of the elm'. Using the words 'female' and 'fingers' implies that she is using this idea in comparison with herself and Bottom. Her exclamatives at the end of the extract also allow the audience to pity her: 'O, how I love thee! How I dote on thee!' It is evident that the charm truly has worked, since she has no reason to feel this way, particularly as he contradicts her 'I had rather have a handful or two of dried pease'.

This effect is emphasised by the fact that it is clear who actually holds more power: although Bottom is governing the conversation, Titania is the more powerful — this is shown in 'Fairies be gone, and be all ways away.' She has given him authority over the fairies, however, which he is shown to accept graciously via his terms of address 'Monsieur' and 'Cavalery Cobweb'. This too creates humour, since it is clear that Bottom is rather out of his depth.

Overall, it is clear that Shakespeare uses a variety of literary and linguistic techniques to convey dramatic effects.

In these final paragraphs, the candidate remains focused on dramatic effect and audience response, describing the likely emotions felt at the Bottom/Titania mismatch, and the poignancy of her passion, expressed in the natural images of the honeysuckle and the ivy and through verbal mood. A clever point is the description of the imagery as 'anthropomorphising' nature.

This answer provides clear and accurate contexts for both passages, with a reasonable amount of detail. The candidate remains strongly aware of dramatic effects and audience response throughout. There is effective reference to the bullet points when focusing on linguistic, literary, discourse and phonological features, and the candidate explains with textual support how they work. He/she links the communication of dramatic emotion with the bullet points, and is aware of humour/comic imagery. More could have been made of discourse patterns, and of the prose/verse variation. Overall, this is a fluent and detailed answer which matches the descriptors for the top 30–35 band. This answer would be awarded 30 marks.

■ ■ ■

Hamlet

Passage A

HAMLET:	My excellent good friends. How dost thou, Guildenstern? Ah, Rosencrantz! Good lads, how do you both?
ROSENCRANTZ:	As the indifferent children of the earth.
GUILDENSTERN:	Happy in that we are not over-happy. On Fortune's cap we are not the very button.
HAMLET:	Nor the soles of her shoes?
ROSENCRANTZ:	Neither, my lord.
HAMLET:	Then you live about her waist, or in the middle of her favours?
GUILDENSTERN:	Faith, her privates, we.
HAMLET:	In the secret parts of Fortune? O, most true! She is a strumpet. What news?
ROSENCRANTZ:	None, my lord, but that the world's grown honest.
HAMLET:	Then is Doomsday near. But your news is not true. Let me question more in particular. What have you, my good friends, deserved at the hands of Fortune that she sends you to prison hither?
GUILDENSTERN:	Prison, my lord?
HAMLET:	Denmark's a prison.

ROSENCRANTZ:	Then is the world one.
HAMLET:	A goodly one; in which there are many confines, wards and dungeons, Denmark being one o' th' worst.
ROSENCRANTZ:	We think not so, my lord.
HAMLET:	Why, then 'tis none to you. For there is nothing either good or bad but thinking makes it so. To me it is a prison.
ROSENCRANTZ:	Why, then your ambition makes it one. 'Tis too narrow for your mind.
HAMLET:	O God, I could be bounded in a nutshell and count myself a king of infinite space, were it not that I have bad dreams.

Passage B

KING:	Laertes, was your father dear to you? Or are you like the painting of a sorrow, A face without a heart?
LAERTES:	Why ask you this?
KING:	Not that I think you did not love your father, But that I know love is begun by time, And that I see, in passages of proof, Time qualifies the spark and fire of it. There lives within the very flame of love A kind of wick or snuff that will abate it, And nothing is at a like goodness still; For goodness, growing to a pleurisy, Dies in his own too-much. That we would do We should do when we would. For this 'would' changes, And hath abatements and delays as many As there are tongues, are hands, are accidents. And then this 'should' is like a spendthrift sigh, That hurts by easing. But to the quick o' th' ulcer — Hamlet comes back. What would you undertake To show yourself in deed your father's son More than in words?
LAERTES:	To cut his throat i' th' church!
KING:	No place, indeed, should murder sanctuarize. Revenge should have no bounds.

C-grade answer

📝 As you read, note that (unlike in the previous answer) this candidate does not deal with passage A and passage B separately, but moves between the two. This seems a less satisfactory approach, because the focus of the answer shifts constantly and the candidate does not make effective use of the bullet points in the question.

Passage A is set in Act 2. Hamlet has discovered the ghost of his father and knows of his murder. The King notices a change in Hamlet's behaviour and sends for Rosencrantz and Guildenstern to speak and spy on Hamlet so as to discover what is wrong. In this passage Hamlet is expressing his feelings of confinement 'Denmarks a prison', he is also showing his supposed madness. This passage points out the lack of difference to the audience between Rosencrantz and Guildenstern, this can be seen in their lack of character and also in the way they speak co-operatively finishing each other's sentences. At the end of this passage Rosencrantz and Guildenstern confirm to the King that they do think Hamlet is mad. The relationship between Hamlet and Rosencrantz and Guildenstern is a friendly one as they are old school friends, their friendship is indicated in 'my excellent good friends' although this is a lie from Hamlet as he knows why Rosencrantz and Guildenstern have come to see him as can be seen after this passage ends.

📝 This paragraph addresses the first bullet point reasonably well but the contexts are not completely accurate (Act II Scene i). Rather than showing madness, Hamlet is behaving perfectly normally here (unlike the previous scene with Polonius). The candidate mentions the audience halfway through the paragraph but fails to describe the comic *effect* of Rosencrantz and Guildenstern's double act. However, Hamlet does not know why Rosencrantz and Guildenstern have come until he becomes suspicious at 'What news?'

In passage B, Laertes is being persuaded by the King to exact revenge for his father's death upon Hamlet. Before this passage Laertes had returned to overthrow and kill the King but the King manages to persuade him otherwise. This passage leads eventually to the duel between Laertes and Hamlet. In passage B, Laertes is seeking revenge for his father's murder and is deeply angered. The King uses his powers of persuasion to get Laertes to kill Hamlet for him.

📝 This context for passage B is clear and accurate.

The purpose of passage A is to show Hamlet's supposed madness and that it may simply be a trick. The passage also shows that Guildenstern and Rosencrantz are not truly Hamlet's friends and are betraying him. The effect of passage A is that it adds to the argument of whether Hamlet is mad or not.

📝 The audience has in fact already seen Hamlet pretending to be mad in the previous scene with Polonius: here he is shown (initially at least) joking with his university friends like any normal young man. This passage confirms to the audience that Hamlet is adopting an 'antic disposition' and is perfectly sane.

The purpose of passage B is to show Laertes anger to the audience and that he is willing to kill Hamlet. Passage B also shows the Kings diplomatic skills in his persuasion of Laertes, this shows to the audience how he came to have his power and position. Shakespeare uses passage B to set up the ending duel between Laertes and Hamlet, indicating to the audience that a conclusion is approaching.

> The candidate makes a successful point in this paragraph about revealing Claudius's character. However, the focus on the purpose of each passage is distracting and would have been better incorporated into the paragraphs on context.

In passage A, Hamlet is of a higher status than Rosencrantz and Guildenstern as he is the Prince of Denmark. Hamlet reflects his higher status through his use of interrogatives, for example 'of her shoe?' and 'What news?' Hamlet makes one of the interrogatives to set the agenda at the start of the passage — this is done to add effect to his feigned madness. At the start, Rosencrantz and Guildenstern are the dominant speakers but this role changes to Hamlet as he becomes more dominant when he begins to describe his confinement. Hamlet adds lexical effect to his feelings of confinement by the use of pattern of three 'confines, wards and dungeons'. Throughout, Hamlet flouts the maxim of relevance. Shakespeare does this to add to the dramatic effect of Hamlet appearing to be mad. The passage is mainly in adjacency pairs with a question being asked and an answer being given. Shakespeare uses this to show the familiarity between Hamlet and Rosencrantz and Guildenstern.

> The inaccurate context starts to cause trouble in this paragraph: contrary to the candidate's statement, up to now Hamlet has not been feigning madness. Although the point about his status being enhanced by his using interrogatives is valid, it could have been explained better, and the truncated quotation is ineffective. There are several points in this paragraph where the candidate makes an unsupported assertion or fails to explain a point, for example, 'Hamlet flouts the maxim of relevance'. It is incorrect to say that Rosencrantz and Guildenstern are dominant. Hamlet sets the agenda and speaks first. 'Triple structure', not 'pattern of three', is the correct rhetorical term.

In passage B the King sets the agenda through his use of interrogatives, thus showing his higher status. This is used by Shakespeare to add to the effect of the King having control over Laertes and using this control to manipulate Laertes into killing Hamlet. The King makes a long speech in poetry to have an emotional effect upon Laertes thus persuading him into killing Hamlet. In the passage the King makes use of figurative language to create imagery as can be seen in the use of 'hurts' and 'ulcer' in which the King is referring to Hamlet. The use of imagery presents Laertes with the idea that if he kills Hamlet his pain shall be eased. The King makes use of rhetorical devices such as questions, 'a face without a heart?' in his changing of agenda.

> There is some confusion in this paragraph, for example, 'figurative language' is an alternative term for 'imagery'. The candidate also fails to comment on the imagery of disease throughout the play. The speech referred to here uses two disease metaphors,

'pleurisy' and 'ulcer', and the candidate loses an opportunity to make a very good point about the play as a whole. There are also points in this paragraph where the candidate should have either used a quotation or extended a truncated one.

The phonological features of passage A are Hamlet's use of exclamatives, showing that the prosodics of the line will be in a loud manner. Exclamatives are also used in passage B to show Laertes's anger 'cut his throat i' th' church!' this indicates the line will be delivered in an aggressive manner. In passage B the King is the dominant speaker.

> ☑ Although exclamatives are a grammatical feature, the candidate is interested in the delivery of the exclamation, so this comment fulfils the fourth bullet point. However, nothing has been said about the change from blank verse to prose in passage A, which signals Hamlet's realisation that Rosencrantz and Guildenstern have not just come on a social visit — this is an important omission.

> ☑ **The candidate is reasonably sound on contexts for both passages, and makes some reference to discourse features, linguistic theory and rhetorical usage, but without much explanation of how they work in the text. Similarly, the candidate notes the use of disease imagery in passage B but does not explain or explore the effect achieved. Although there is occasional mention of audience, there is little steady focus on dramatic effects or how they are created. Overall, this is a knowledgeable but under-developed answer. There is some identification of features, and sufficient explanation is provided to ensure that the answer is placed in the 18–23 band. This answer would be awarded a mark of 20, but more attention to dramatic effects, less repetition and more textual support would merit the award of a significantly higher mark.**

■ ■ ■

In the following two sections, short extracts have been taken from *Twelfth Night* and *The School for Scandal*, and a model answer is provided for each. The structure of the answers follows the order of the bullet points in Question 1.

Twelfth Night

VIOLA: The honourable lady of the house, which is she?

OLIVIA: Speak to me, I shall answer for her. Your will?

VIOLA: Most radiant, exquisite and unmatchable beauty — I pray you, tell me if this be the lady of the house, for I never saw her. I would be loath to cast away

> my speech; for besides that it is excellently well penned, I have taken great pains to con it. Good beauties, let me sustain no scorn. I am very comptible, even to the least sinister usage.
>
> OLIVIA: Whence came you, sir?
>
> VIOLA: I can say little more than I have studied, and that question's out of my part. Good gentle one, give me modest assurance if you be lady of the house, that I may proceed in my speech.
>
> OLIVIA: Are you a comedian?
>
> VIOLA: No, my profound heart; and yet, by the very fangs of malice, I swear I am not that I play. Are you the lady of the house?
>
> OLIVIA: If I do not usurp myself, I am.
>
> VIOLA: Most certain, if you are she, you do usurp yourself; for what is yours to bestow is not yours to reserve. But this is from my commission. I will on with my speech in your praise, and then show you the heart of my message.
>
> OLIVIA: Come to what is important in't. I forgive you the praise.
>
> VIOLA: Alas, I took great pains to study it, and 'tis poetical.
>
> OLIVIA: It is the more likely to be feigned; I pray you, keep it in. I heard you were saucy at my gates, and allowed your approach rather to wonder at you than to hear you. If you be not mad, be gone; if you have reason, be brief. 'Tis not that time of the moon with me, to make one in so skipping a dialogue.
>
> MARIA: *[Showing Viola the way out]* Will you hoist sail, sir? Here lies your way.
>
> VIOLA: No, good swabber, I am to hull here a little longer.

Model answer

The first paragraph addresses context and makes brief reference to the play as a whole.

Shipwrecked Viola, in male disguise, has entered Duke Orsino's service, and has been ordered to woo the lady Olivia for him. In this scene, Olivia (against her better judgement) is attracted by Viola's wit and charm. The humour for the audience is that both are deceived (Olivia does not know Viola is a woman; Viola is completely unaware of her own attractiveness). The potential for confusion later in the play is enhanced by the fact that Orsino is equally deceived and equally charmed by Viola, and also that Viola is falling in love with him. Immediately before Viola's entrance, the audience has seen Malvolio's determined attempt to keep her away from Olivia. The passage establishes for the audience the wit of both women. It raises some questions about the nature of true love (relevant later in the play) through the comedy of Viola's studied courtship.

question

📝 The next two paragraphs focus on the dramatic effects produced by spoken language features and discourse conventions.

Following the initial rapid adjacency pair, the exchange between the two women seems to be dominated by Viola's longer turns, despite Olivia's higher status as lady of the house. Nevertheless, Olivia asks most of the questions ('Your will?', 'Whence came you, sir?', 'Are you a comedian?') and in effect sets the agenda, showing the audience her personal status and power. Viola's power lies in her wit ('No, good swabber') and in the amusing transition from the speech she learnt ('Most radiant, exquisite and unmatchable beauty') and her informal comment 'I would be loath to cast away my speech; for besides that it is excellently well penned, I have taken great pains to con it.'

The audience, well aware of Viola's true identity ('I swear I am not that I play') is entertained not only by the growing misunderstanding but also by Viola's sprightly courage in her new role. Her chosen terms of address are eloquent and perhaps slightly comic to the audience ('Most radiant...', 'Good beauties', 'Good gentle one'). In contrast, the audience almost starts when Viola is addressed as 'Sir', having nearly forgotten her disguise. In terms of the power balance, honours are about even, because Olivia's curiosity is so piqued that she is reluctant to send Viola away, despite their unequal status. A final discourse feature which confirms their equal social status is reflected in their usage of the formal 'you'.

📝 This next paragraph shows how literary, grammatical and rhetorical features create dramatic effects.

There is an amusing mix of register and lexical choice in this passage, drawing the audience's attention to the artifice of Orsino's dramatic passion. The hyperbolic triple structure mentioned already ('Most radiant, exquisite and unmatchable beauty') is a fine example of the dramatic use of rhetoric. Similarly effective are the use of antithesis ('what is yours to bestow is not yours to reserve') and syntactic parallelism ('if you be not mad, be gone; if you have reason, be brief'). Viola and Olivia both use less formal lexis ('I have taken great pains to con it', 'I heard you were saucy at my gates'); and Viola also makes effective use of ship-related imagery ('I am to hull here a little longer'), although the metaphor 'by the very fangs of malice' has a sinister note to it, presaging darker events ahead. Viola uses polite mitigated directives to Olivia 'I pray you, tell me' as well as the direct key question 'Are you the lady of the house?' Her confident declaratives show that she is presenting as solid a case as possible: 'I will on with my speech of praise'. Olivia is much more terse, inclined to question and use imperatives (all conveying her superior status). The whole exchange creates for the audience a rich and sharp brew, colourful, varied and witty, and revealing something about each character.

📝 This paragraph focuses on the dramatic use of phonological features, including delivery of lines in performance.

One of the most significant performance aspects of this passage is its pace. The overall impression is one of wit and good humour. Olivia, still mourning her brother, has just invited Feste to cheer her with his 'good fooling' and is thus prepared to indulge Viola's repartee. The combination of wit, wordplay ('if I do not usurp myself', 'if you are she you do usurp yourself') and rapid riposte ('I forgive you the praise') creates an excited and tense mood in the audience. Even though the whole extract is in prose, the rhythmic beat of antithesis, balanced structures, synthetic parallelism and short and long utterances powers the scene onwards towards the moment when Olivia agrees to listen to Orsino's wooing. There is some alliteration and assonance ('sustain no scorn' 'hoist, here, hull sail, sir, swabber'), but the internal rhythms of speech carry the exchange onwards, including the adjacency pairs structure underlying the whole exchange, regardless of differing lengths of turn.

This richly patterned scene offers great opportunities for actors who enjoy well-honed repartee, and it shows the audience how similar these women are (though seemingly different). Ironically, disguised Viola is a more successful wooer of Olivia than Orsino. This makes it slightly more credible later in the play that Olivia should fall in love with her twin Sebastian, and he with her.

■ ■ ■

The School for Scandal

[Lady Sneerwell's dressing room. Lady Sneerwell discovered at the dressing table; Snake drinking chocolate.]

LADY SNEERWELL: The paragraphs, you say, Mr Snake, were all inserted?

SNAKE: They were, madam; and, as I copied them myself in a feigned hand, there can be no suspicion whence they came.

LADY SNEERWELL: Did you circulate the report of Lady Brittle's intrigue with Captain Boastall?

SNAKE: That's in as fine a train as your ladyship could wish. In the common course of things, I think it must reach Mrs Clackitt's ears within four-and-twenty hours; and then, you know, the business is as good as done.

LADY SNEERWELL: Why, truly, Mrs Clackitt has a very pretty talent — and a great deal of industry.

SNAKE: True, madam, and has been tolerably successful in her day. To my knowledge, she has been the cause of six matches being broken off,

question

> and three sons being disinherited, of four forced elopements, as many close confinements, nine separate maintenances, and two divorces. Nay, I have more than once traced her causing a *tête-à-tête* in the *Town and Country Magazine*, when the parties, perhaps, had never seen each other's face before in the course of their lives.
>
> LADY SNEERWELL: She certainly has talents, but her manner is gross.
>
> SNAKE: 'Tis very true. She generally designs well, has a free tongue and a bold invention; but her colouring is too dark and her outlines often extravagant. She wants that delicacy of hint and mellowness of sneer which distinguishes your ladyship's scandal.
>
> LADY SNEERWELL: Ah, you are partial, Snake.
>
> SNAKE: Not in the least. Everybody allows that Lady Sneerwell can do more with a word or look than many can with the most laboured detail, even when they happen to have a little truth on their side to support it. [*They rise.*]
>
> LADY SNEERWELL: Yes, my dear Snake; and I am no hypocrite to deny the satisfaction I reap from the success of my efforts. Wounded myself in the early part of my life by the envenomed tongue of slander, I confess I have since known no pleasure equal to the reducing others to the level of my own injured reputation.
>
> SNAKE: Nothing can be more natural.

Model answer

The first paragraph focuses on context, including a brief reference to the play as a whole.

This extract comes from the opening of the play, so the context inevitably looks forward not backward; the audience needs to be prepared for potential themes, characters and plot. The exchange between Snake and Lady Sneerwell takes place in her private rooms, where she is putting the finishing touches to her appearance. The audience would recognise this as normal practice in the higher echelons of society. It is immediately clear that Snake and Lady Sneerwell are fellow conspirators in their passion to spread scandal, and the rationale for their behaviour is given by Lady Sneerwell ('Wounded myself...by the envenomed tongue of slander...I have known no other pleasure equal to the reducing others to the level of my own injured reputation'). The audience now has a sense of character (assisted by the carefully stereotyped names) and of potential plot (personal lives destroyed or turned upside down by rumour and scandal). The theme of corruption is also established clearly, in that neither Snake nor Lady Sneerwell has any moral repugnance for the harm scandal brings — indeed, she positively gains 'pleasure' from it. The fact that truth and factual accuracy are of no interest to Snake or Lady Sneerwell suggests to the audience that the play in some way will set up an opposition between scandal and lies and truth and honour. The rest of this scene continues the theme of corruption, and it is not until the beginning of Scene 2 that a more honourable (though flawed) character, Sir Peter Teazle, is introduced.

The second paragraph explores the dramatic effects achieved by spoken language features and discourse conventions.

This is an entirely harmonious, even sycophantic exchange, with the middle-class Snake conspiring with the aristocratic Lady Sneerwell. The terms of address (though appropriate to the formal style of polite society in the eighteenth century) do suggest some social distance between the speakers ('Mr Snake', 'madam', 'your ladyship'). Interestingly, Lady Sneerwell varies from a haughty 'Snake' to a seemingly friendly 'my dear Snake'. The discourse structure starts with adjacency pairs and Lady Sneerwell is the interrogator. Once her questions have been resolved, she and Snake comment antiphonally (like alternating choristers in a very secular church) on the scandal-spreading achievements of the remarkable Mrs Clackitt. Snake flatters Lady Sneerwell about her superior skills as a scandalmonger. The scene is set for the 'school for scandal'. The effect on the audience of this exchange is to shock and amuse equally — the laughter is likely to be a little uncomfortable at the human misery, hypocrisy and corruption exposed or enacted as a result of Mrs Clackitt's gossiping. The irony that truth and falsehood are hard to distinguish comes across clearly.

The third paragraph focuses on the dramatic effectiveness of literary, grammatical and rhetorical features.

The most obvious literary devices at work are metaphor ('the envenomed tongue of slander') and personification ('Snake' and 'Sneerwell' present unpleasant images to the audience, 'Snake' suggesting poison and deceit, and 'Sneerwell' suggesting the corruption of pride, vanity and arrogance). When Lady Sneerwell explains the reason for her scandalmongering, a further motive (revenge) confirms the cruel and destructive power implied by 'sneer [ing] well'. Other personified names are more amusing to the audience ('Lady Brittle'— a trivial woman; 'Captain Boastall' — an unattractive blustering kind of man). The remarkably 'talented' scandalmonger is well-named 'Mrs Clackitt', the onomatopoeia suggesting busy tongues wagging and tapping on teeth, jaws clicking and mouths muttering. The rhetorical device of listing Mrs Clackitt's 'achievements' is dramatically effective because it is simultaneously amusing and horrifying ('six matches...broken, three sons disinherited, four elopements, four secret confinements, nine maintenances and two divorces'). Snake's unfavourable comparing of Mrs Clackitt and Lady Sneerwell is syntactically elegant, if cruel. An opening triple structure ('designs well...free tongue...bold invention') is balanced ('but') against two elaborate — and flattering — noun phrases, referring to Lady Sneerwell's 'delicacy of hint and mellowness of sneer'. The fact that Mrs Clackitt's slandering is likened to the art of painting ('her colouring...too dark...her outlines

...extravagant') shows the audience the level of moral corruption in this world. And yet we all laugh!

2 The fourth paragraph focuses on phonological features, pace and delivery of lines in performance.

The delivery of these plays of social manners needs to be fast-paced and lively, and never slow and portentous. The morality (or otherwise) of the action has to sweep the audience along, even though its members despise what they laugh at. Hyperbole is at the heart of this play — and yet it cannot be delivered in an exaggerated 'knowing' way or the humour will be killed, and the moral framework supporting the play will disappear. In other words, actors must take their parts entirely seriously. So this opening scene, with all its outrageousness, has to be played straight and fast. This is assisted by the varied turn-taking, and probably by the audience's shocked but amused collusion with this portrait of contemporary society. Sheridan is skilful in his ability to recreate the rhythms of colloquial speech ('Nay, I have more than once traced her', 'tis very true', 'Ah, you are partial, Snake').

This passage introduces the contemporary audience to a satirical view of upper-class eighteenth-century society. For the modern audience, the themes of scandal and scandalmongering are embodied in the characters Snake and Lady Sneerwell in a comic but shocking way, since they make such outrageous assumptions about their privileged world. Sheridan exploits his sharp ear for language, and particularly 'high society', and succeeds brilliantly — even if the audience is made a little uncomfortable.

Question 2: unseen texts

Doctor–patient consultation and extract from *Middlemarch*

Text A is an extract from a transcribed consultation between a doctor (D) and a patient (P).

Text B is an extract from the novel *Middlemarch* (1872) by George Eliot. Mr Casaubon, an elderly scholar and clergyman, has requested a consultation with the doctor, Mr Lydgate. Dorothea is Mr Casaubon's young wife. Mr Casaubon fears that his ill health might interfere with the completion of his lifelong work.

Compare the two texts, commenting on the ways in which they reflect differences and similarities between talk in real life and talk in literature.

You should refer in your answer to:
- the significance of context and situation
- the functions of interaction
- how attitudes and values are conveyed

Text A

PATIENT:	what it is er I work with elderly people
DOCTOR:	yeh
PATIENT:	and yesterday I got home from work and *[inaudible]* the trouble is I can't bend forward and I can't like turn sideways it's like the bottom of my spine it just feels I'm sitting on a pin
DOCTOR:	so it's pain in the lower back
PATIENT:	lower back just about there
DOCTOR:	OK how long did you say again
PATIENT:	I mean all last night I couldn't turn on my side I couldn't stand up I couldn't go to the toilet
DOCTOR:	so it got worse overnight
PATIENT:	yeh when I walk it hurts me to walk (.) I don't know what it I don't know if probably it's lifting the residents in the nursing home or what
DOCTOR:	no remembered injury (.) you don't remember doing anything in particular

PATIENT: I've I've worked with elderly people for 10 years moving them around

DOCTOR: waterworks OK

PATIENT: yeh fine

DOCTOR: can you climb on the couch while I have a look at your back just lie flat on your back

PATIENT: lie back oh ooh *[inaudible]*

DOCTOR: I'll give you a hand (.) just relax back as best as you can (.) sorry (.) as you are comfortable OK

PATIENT: yeh

DOCTOR: it's when you move

PATIENT: it's when I move and when I lie on my bed back in the house I can't lie straight I have to lift my bottom up otherwise I can feel something like ripping the back of my spine

DOCTOR: what I want you to do first then is to press down with your feet against my hands press down hard (.) OK now pull up against my fingers (.) can you press your feet together press your knees apart (.) just relax while I do your reflexes which are fine (.) can you bend your knees

PATIENT: oh

DOCTOR: yes OK take your time (.) now keep them as they are while I just try and straighten your legs (.) right now let your feet come down that's it (.) I'm going to do the work if you can try and relax and tell me when it gets too uncomfortable

PATIENT: now

DOCTOR: that's it OK so about 40 degrees (.) now *[inaudible]* now this one

PATIENT: there

DOCTOR: about the same (.) can I sit you forward now while I while I hit you

PATIENT: *[laughs: inaudible]* that's as far as I can't go any further

DOCTOR: tell me where the tender spot is

PATIENT: there oh

DOCTOR: er further down

PATIENT: no just there

DOCTOR: no (.) sides

PATIENT: yeh

DOCTOR:	so that's the worse spreading out to both sides
PATIENT:	yeh
DOCTOR:	let your feet hang over the edge
PATIENT:	never had this before
DOCTOR:	come and sit yourself down (.) sorry I'll move that out of the way
PATIENT:	I thought I'd better come to the doctor because with me working with residents I thought well I don't want to put my back out
DOCTOR:	er no you can't work like this at the moment you find that any movement catches it so lifting people is just out at the moment (.) I'm sure this is a muscle tear because it's typical of them that er the time you do it you don't feel much it's often overnight that the pain steadily develops
PATIENT:	I was coming home from work and I only seemed to feel it when I got in last night when I got into the warmth (.) it was all right at the time (.) I've been in agony all night
DOCTOR:	so the first thing is rest (.) secondly I'll give you some painkillers they don't speed up the healing it's just to make life comfortable for you while it's healing

Text B

'You refer to the possible hindrances from want of health?' [Mr Lydgate] said, wishing to help forward Mr Casaubon's purpose, which seemed to be clogged by some hesitation.

'I do. You have not implied to me that the symptoms which — I am bound to testify — you watched with scrupulous care, were those of a fatal disease. But were it so, Mr Lydgate, I should desire to know the truth without reservation, and I appeal to you for an exact statement of your conclusions: I request it as a friendly service. If you can tell me that my life is not threatened by anything else than ordinary casualties, I shall rejoice, on grounds which I have already indicated. If not, knowledge of the truth is even more important to me.'

'Then I can no longer hesitate as to my course,' said Lydgate; 'but the first thing I must impress on you is that my conclusions are doubly uncertain — uncertain not only because of my fallibility, but because diseases of the heart are eminently difficult to found predictions on. In any case, one can hardly increase appreciably the tremendous uncertainty of life.'

Mr Casaubon winced perceptibly, but bowed.

'I believe that you are suffering from what is called fatty degeneration of the heart, a disease which was first divined and explored by Laennec, the man who gave us the stethoscope, not so very many years ago. A good deal of experience — a more lengthened observation — is wanted on the subject. But after what you have said, it is my duty to tell you that death from this disease is often sudden. At the same time, no such result can be predicted. Your condition may be consistent with a tolerably comfortable life for another fifteen years, or even more. I could add no information to this, beyond anatomical or medical details, which would leave expectation at precisely the same point.'

Lydgate's instinct was fine enough to tell him that plain speech, quite free from ostentatious caution, would be felt by Mr Casaubon as a tribute of respect.

'I thank you, Mr Lydgate,' said Mr Casaubon, after a moment's pause. 'One thing more I have still to ask: did you communicate what you have now told me to Mrs Casaubon?'

'Partly — I mean, as to the possible issues.' Lydgate was going to explain why he had told Dorothea, but Mr Casaubon, with an unmistakable desire to end the conversation, waved his hand slightly, and said again, 'I thank you.'

Lydgate, certain that his patient wished to be alone, soon left him; and the black figure with hands behind and head bent forward continued to pace the walk where the dark yew-trees gave him a mute companionship in melancholy, and the little shadows of birds or leaf that fleeted across the isles of sunlight, stole along in silence as in the presence of a sorrow.

A-grade answer

In texts A and B, the differences and similarities between talk in life and talk in literature are shown in various ways. The context of both is that they both have patients visiting their doctor to be diagnosed and treated. In both cases the doctor has the information and tries to help and explain the condition as clearly as possible. Both patients want to be diagnosed truthfully — because text A is a transcript of a real consultation we know the doctor will tell the truth, B is less certain because it is from a novel and so for dramatic tension, Eliot could have chosen to withhold the information.

🖉 The candidate establishes comparison immediately by referring to similarities in context, purpose and the obligations of doctors, and shows awareness that genre difference means that a novelist has the power to craft and change things if desired.

The main difference between the patients' situations is that one patient has a small treatable injury of back pain, whereas Mr Casaubon's condition is far more serious, especially because at the time it was written, heart disease would have been fatal.

The relationship between the doctors and patients of the two texts also seems to be slightly different. In text A there is no evidence that the two people have ever met before in their lives. The consultation is very business-like and they do not discuss anything other than the problem at hand — the patient's back pain. However in text B there seems to be more of a relationship between the characters perhaps not friend-ship exactly, but the way in which Mr Lydgate knows Mr Casaubon's wife 'Dorothea' on a first name basis shows they know each other as Mr Casaubon asks 'Did you communicate what you...to Mrs Casaubon?' The fact that the doctor may have spoken to the patient's wife also suggests more of a relationship — this of course is planned by Eliot.

✍ In this paragraph, the candidate contrasts the degree or severity of injury/illness in the two patients — this prepares for comments on attitudes and values later. He/she also implies awareness of the genre of medical consultation, and shows a clear under-standing of the crafted nature of literature. The comment about the relationship between Lydgate and Casaubon is a perfectly valid conclusion within the context of the passage, though the candidate misreads the reference to 'Dorothea' which is in the narrative voice, not Lydgate's. The next two paragraphs compare and explore function and purpose in the two texts.

Because text A is a transcript, the speech is spontaneous and unplanned. This is why there are inaudible utterances, fillers such as 'er' and noises such as 'laughter'. The function of both interactions is to get a diagnosis/information/treatment from the doctor. Because text A is a real situation and so spontaneous, the doctor asks questions as they come to him such as 'so it got worse overnight' and 'you don't remember doing anything in particular'. The doctor is trying to get as much infor-mation as possible so is able to help the patient. These unplanned spontaneous questions will help him to do this. He uses imperatives such as 'lie back' and 'take your time' because he values the patient's health and does not want his condition to get worse. The patient's attitude also seems to be that he is worried about his health as he/she states 'I thought I'd better come...don't want to put my back out'. The main function of the interaction is to get to the bottom of the problem, which is why the doctor examines him.

✍ At the beginning of this paragraph, the candidate focuses on the function and purpose of the exchange and explains it clearly. However, he/she could have found more textual evidence to support the implied attitudes (doctor concerned and supportive, patient anxious) later in the paragraph.

The function of the interaction in text B is very different. Because it is from a novel it means that the text is planned, structured and crafted carefully for dramatic purposes. Although I have not read the novel, I think the purpose of this interaction is to move the plot along, as one of the main characters who is elderly with a young wife discovering he has a fatal illness seems to be a main storyline and probably crucial to the book.

2

question

This is a strong comparison of the differing function and purpose of the interaction in text B — the candidate, though very much aware of authorial purpose in B, could have been more explicit about the use of crafting to reveal character.

Unlike in text A, we do not see the doctor, Mr Lydgate, examine Mr Casaubon (presumably he has done this already) but like in text A, the main point of the interaction is to give a diagnosis, which he does 'I believe that you are suffering...degeneration of the heart'. Because the speech is crafted, Eliot uses the interaction to build up tension with Mr Lydgate's speech before 'I must impress on you...found predictions on.' It gives the reader a clue that the news is not good and so Eliot has also used the interaction to create an atmosphere of doom. He does this again at the end of the text where he describes 'the presence of sorrow'.

It is acceptable when quoting a long passage to indicate omissions with a series of dots. In this paragraph, the candidate notes another literary purpose of text B by identifying Eliot's creation of 'an atmosphere of doom'. In the next paragraph, the candidate begins a focused comparison of attitudes and values.

The attitudes and values of text B are also different to that of text A. Because the condition of the patient in text A is not fatal, his attitude is that he does not want it to get any worse. In text B however, Mr Casaubon has just been told that 'death from this disease is often sudden'. When Mr Lydgate is giving his diagnosis, Eliot has used pauses to give the effect of real talk, as if he is trying to get across that the doctor is saying the words gently and slowly to try and reduce their impact.

The candidate could have provided more textual support to confirm the comment on the patient's attitude (shown as concerned and needy). A clearer explanation of Lydgate's concerned attitude is given, and evidence is provided. In the next paragraph Mr Casaubon's fearfulness is also shown.

Mr Casaubon's attitude seems to be that he wants to know the truth about his illness, however bad it may be: 'knowledge of the truth...to me'. Like text A's patient, he values his health and 'winced perceptibly' before being told. Eliot has done this to show perhaps that his character is scared and has carefully crafted this suggestion carefully to come just before the fatal diagnosis.

I think that the thing Mr Casaubon values most is his wife. He asks 'did you communicate...Mrs Casaubon?' I think this shows that he doesn't want his wife to get upset about his condition and wishes to protect her as much as possible from the bad news of his condition. This could be because she is younger.

The candidate focuses immediately on a comparison of the texts, and having established clear differences and similarities in context and situation, addresses differences in genre and purpose promptly, showing a sophisticated understanding of literary and authorial purposes in particular. Because the candidate identifies the genre difference early in the answer, his/her arguments and textual reference support each other. A thoughtful

interpretation of how attitudes and values are conveyed in text **B** is provided, and of ways in which tension is created. This is a clear, concise, intelligent reading of both texts, which addresses all the bullet points and sustains a careful comparison. This answer would be placed in the top band (30–35 marks) and would be awarded 33 marks.

■ ■ ■

C-grade answer

The context of both texts greatly influences the formality of the scene. As both texts are set in a doctor's surgery or room the two characters in each are doctor and patient. Both texts consist of three part exchanges and negative and positive evaluations.

✍ The candidate identifies discourse features but fails to explain why they would appear in doctor–patient exchanges — he/she seems unaware of the genre of professional consultation. The candidate also fails to explain either context and states inaccurately that Lydgate sees Mr Casaubon in a doctor's surgery or room. Another serious error is to describe the speakers in both texts as 'characters' — this applies only to the literary text B.

A distinct difference between the two is the style. Text A is straightforward the reader picks up meaning from adjectives said in conversation. Whereas in text B, talk in literature, the reader receives meaning from the intertwined narrative

✍ These points are elliptical and unclear, since 'style' is really only applicable to a literary text. In the paragraph below, the term 'stylised' should be 'crafted'.

Talk in literature is stylised, and the narrative thematic so the writer can reveal the context through narration, however in talk in life, context is signalled through key words, such as 'tender spot' and 'lie down'. Talk in life, as in text A is made up greatly of three part exchanges and elicitations — questions or commands that are asked to get a response. Whereas in text B is narration that unfolds the story.

✍ The candidate seems to suggest that lexical field reveals context in spontaneous talk, but the examples given are not necessarily convincing. Although he/she picks out linguistic features, these one-sentence comparisons do not help to develop the candidate's argument because no explanations are given.

Text A is full of pauses and hesitations such as 'like' this is so the speaker has time to think about what is said next, whereas in text B the dialogue is very smooth, precise and pre-thought. Talk in life requires supportive responses to urge the speaker on, those in text A are presented by markers such as 'yeh' and 'OK' whereas in talk in literature there is little need for these as the narrator bridges these gaps with narration a response then is really straight after.

✍ Again, there is feature-spotting comparison here with no real discussion. The candidate notes the use of contracted forms and links them to register and levels of formality,

then refers briefly to linguistic theory before returning to generalisations about talk in literature. So far, only linguistic points have been supported by textual evidence.

In talk in life in text A, both the doctor and the patient contract their words and use elision to reveal thoughts, for example 'yeh' and 'gonna'. This is a common feature of everyday talk and resembles how conversation has seen the formality of language change over time. However talk in literature is stylised and so the characters' speech in text B is formalised purposely. This is likely because the writer feels interaction between a high status doctor and a 'normal' patient should be formal as a politeness principle. Talk in literature allows the writer's attitudes and values to be revealed in this way.

Another example of how talk in literature differs from talk in life is the doctor's use of terms of address. Mr Lydgate addresses his patient by name whereas the doctor in text A does not. This is because in real life conversation, doctors tend not to call their patients by name and tend to get the job done as fast as possible. Talk in life reveals how social situations really are whereas talk in literature can be planned, and staged to how the writer wants it to be — this is evidence of the speaker's and writer's values.

🖉 In this paragraph, the candidate fails to explain the formality of the doctor's use of terms of address, and makes generalisations which would be more valuable if supported by textual examples.

Context also affects the differences between the two types of conversation. For example text B is represented as having an older setting than text A as there are references to the recently invented stethoscope, this setting affects how much information needs to be revealed for a reader or audience to understand. However in text A there is no reference to any medical equipment. A likely reason for this is because people in real-life talk do not have to make anyone understand other than the other participant in conversation. For example, attitudes are revealed through paralinguistic features such as in text A '(laughs)'. By using these the doctor understands the patient whereas in talk in literature the characters are not real and the fundamental purpose is that the readers understand.

🖉 The candidate moves from commenting on social context to generalised comments on attitudes to patients.

Also rarely in real-life talk do people flaunt their vocabulary, simple adjectives such as text A's 'pain' reveal the problem whereas in text B vocabulary such as 'eminently' and 'fallibility' are used. Talk in literature is stylised in this way to reveal status and make the story more interesting.

🖉 The candidate comments on the difference in the speakers' lexical choices, but does not point out that words like 'fallibility' fit the more formal register of a nineteenth-century fictional exchange.

Text A is full of pauses as the speaker awaits a response from the doctor, or to think about what to say next, these are common features of spontaneous talk, however in text B there is none, this shows the differences between different types of talk, because talk in literature is planned and is a story.

🖉 This point of comparison is not valid — there are pauses in text B. It is also very late to be commenting on purposes — these should have been noted much earlier in the answer, preferably in conjunction with discussion of genre.

Similarities between the two texts are the topics dealt with in talk in this particular context. In text A the issue of the patient's job arises as it does too in text B. Both doctors use a heuristic function to find out information about their patient. Also in both texts the doctor seems to hold the floor, with the patient initiating the appropriate responses, this is the same in real life and in literature because of the status of the doctor.

🖉 The candidate should be commenting on what is actually present in these texts, not what he/she expects to be there.

In both texts there is elements of phatic talk simply to bridge the gap of between patient and doctor to make their relationship seem more personal. Talk in literature text B reveals more emotions and feelings than text A does, text A does not do this as in real life people who do not know each other rarely reveal their feelings other than symptoms as relevant to the context of the situation.

🖉 The candidate makes several unsupported assertions in this paragraph.

Talk in literature often follows Labov's structure of story with a beginning a middle and an end. However, talk in real life rarely does this as it does not follow rules.

🖉 This a risky generalisation since Labov's theory is based on spoken, not written, narrative. In any case, it is far too late in the essay to introduce new theoretical perspectives.

🖉 **Because the candidate did not address the genre difference between a spontaneous and a crafted text in the opening paragraph, the comparisons throughout are based on feature-spotting, and these features are explained in terms of context, function or purpose. The candidate is simply comparing two sorts of conversation/dialogue by describing the texts, but not analysing them. The comments on attitudes and values tend to be generalised, rather than being supported by the text. Though clearly knowledgeable about spoken discourse features, the candidate seems unable to relate this understanding to both texts, and is specific only about text A. There is some understanding of the differences and similarities between spoken and crafted speech, but the initial missed opportunities lead to a series of random-seeming comparisons which are rather unconvincing. This answer is at the lower end of the 18–23 band and would be awarded 18 marks.**

■ ■ ■

In the following section, two extracts from monologues (a transcript and part of a poem) have been selected, and a model answer provided. This answer follows the structure of the bullet points in Question 2.

Visit to family and 'A Servant to Servants'

Text A is the transcribed account of a visit made by the speaker (Anna) and her aunt to the house where the aunt spent her childhood. During the visit, Aunty Sheila was recognised by Anna's great uncle, whom she had not seen since childhood. Anna is telling her women friends about the visit.

Text B is the beginning of 'A Servant to Servants', a narrative poem by the American poet Robert Frost. The female narrator lives on a New England farm, and is talking to a visitor to her home.

Compare the two texts, commenting on the ways in which they reflect differences and similarities between a single speaker telling her story in real life, and the representation of a single speaker telling her story in literature.

You should refer in your answer to:
- **the significance of context and situation**
- **point of view and narrative structure**
- **how attitudes and values are conveyed**

Text A

Ooh I didn't tell you about my trip to Derby did I? Last weekend with Aunty Sheila and Jessie. It was so funny. This was — I took my aunt, my father's sister, really our only surviving relative that we know about, to Derby, because that's where she and my father grew up. *[passage omitted]* And just on the off-chance she took me to this little village called Fairfield. Now my father always used to talk about Fairfield Hall where my great-grandfather lived when my dad was a child *[passage omitted]*. So we went to Fairfield, and we went to look for Fairfield Hall *[passage omitted]*. And I'd pictured this great big house on top of a hill with a big gravel drive, and it wasn't like that at all. It was just a very very nice Georgian — very big Georgian country house with a relatively short gravel drive, and nothing — particularly like I'd imagined. And we had a look, and thought it was very interesting, and we were all getting back into the car *[passage omitted]* and Aunty Sheila said 'Are you not going to knock on the door then?' and I said 'No. No, I don't think so.' And then I thought — but then I thought, 'Hang on a minute — why not?' you know. The worst that could happen is that they could be really rude and slam the door shut and yell 'Go away'. So I said 'OK let's go and see.' *[passage omitted]* So we walked up to the front door, and I-I rang the bell, and this man answered the door who was about my aunt's age, and I said 'I'm sorry to bother you but are there any members of the Lamb family still living here?'

And that was the family surname then, and he looked at me, and he said 'Why do you ask?' And then he looked at my aunt and he said 'Are you Tezhy?' And Tezhy was her nickname as a little girl. It was short for Treasure, really obnoxious. You can imagine. She — she was a little girl in the thirties with those silly dresses and a big bow on the side of them. And this happens to be Bruno who's like a great uncle of mine. Bruno Skinner his name was. And he recognised Aunty Sheila and he said 'Come in, come in', and he took us into the house. *[passage omitted]* I just thought it was really strange to sit in this room in this house that had been in the family for like a hundred years, and to think that my dad had played there as a child, and my grandfather and all these people — all these people — who I've got photographs of, and I've only heard of their lives through snatches of stories *[passage omitted]* and it was really strange.

Text B

I didn't make you know how glad I was
To have you come and camp here on our land.
I promised myself to get down some day
And see the way you lived, but I don't know!
With a houseful of hungry men to feed
I guess you'd find...It seems to me
I can't express my feelings any more
Than I can raise my voice or want to lift
My hand (oh, I can lift it when I have to).
Did ever you feel so? I hope you never.
It's got so I don't even know for sure
Whether I *am* glad, sorry or anything.
There's nothing left but a voice-like left inside
That seems to tell me how I ought to feel,
And would feel if I wasn't all gone wrong.
You take the lake. I look and look at it.
I see it's a fair, pretty sheet of water.
I stand and make myself repeat out loud
The advantages it has, so long and narrow,
Like a deep piece of some old running river
Cut short off at both ends. It lies five miles
Straight away through the mountain notch
From the sink window where I wash the plates,
And all our storms come up toward the house,
Drawing the slow waves whiter and whiter and whiter.
It took my mind off doughnuts and soda biscuit
To step outdoors and take the water dazzle
A sunny morning, or take the rising wind

> About my face and body and through my wrapper,
> When a storm threatened from the Dragon's Den,
> And a cold chill shivered across the lake.
> I see it's a fair, pretty sheet of water,
> Our Willoughby! How did you hear of it?
> I expect, though, everyone's heard of it.
> In a book about ferns? Listen to that!
> You let things more like feathers regulate
> Your going and coming. And you like it here?
> I can see how you might. But I don't know!
> It would be different if more people came,
> For then there would be business. As it is,
> The cottages Len built, sometimes we rent them,
> Sometimes we don't. We've a good piece of shore
> That ought to be worth something, and may yet.
> But I don't count on it as much as Len.
> He looks on the bright side of everything,
> Including me. He thinks I'll be all right
> With doctoring. But it's not medicine —
> Lowe is the only doctor's dared to say so —
> It's rest I want — there, I have said it out —
> From cooking meals for hungry hired men
> And washing dishes after them — from doing
> Things over and over that just won't stay done.

Model answer

🖉 The first paragraphs explain the significance of context and situation.

The basic comparison here is between two women telling a personal story to friendly listeners. The age of the women is not specified, but the speaker in text A seems relatively young, while the speaker in text B is probably middle-aged. Although both texts appear to be monologues, there are unnamed addressees in both contexts ('You can imagine' and 'And you like it here?'). The personal stories differ: in text A, a specific episode in the recent past is narrated and some further reference made to other family history; in text B the story is an individual personal history — almost a Puritan self-examination.

The difference in genre and purpose is clear — in text A the speaker is telling a story to entertain the audience; in text B the poet is creating through the narrative voice a vivid picture of the exhausting struggle of New England farm life, and the speaker's longing for 'rest' (or death?).

The transcript has the normal non-fluency features characterising spontaneous speech: repetition ('a very very nice Georgian — very big Georgian country house');

hesitations, false starts, self-repairs ('She — she was a little girl'); hedges ('you know' 'for like a hundred years'). The narrative poem, however, though crafted to seem like natural speech ('I guess you'd find', 'Did ever you feel so?'), has no non-fluency features. And although the unrhymed iambic pentameter matches the rhythms of natural speech very closely, it has a smoothness and flow unlike the jerky narrative in text A.

▨ The next paragraphs explore the point of view and narrative structure of the texts.

The narrative point of view in text A is mainly Anna's, though there is a suggestion occasionally that Aunty Sheila or Great Uncle Bruno had their own perspective. The narrative structure follows the Labov pattern (*abstract*: 'my trip to Derby'; *orientation*: 'last weekend with Aunty Sheila'; *complicating action or narrative* visit; *evaluation*: Fairfield Hall and its associations; *result*: 'to think my dad played there...'; *coda*: 'it was really strange'). Text B has a different kind of narrative structure, based on the emotional perspective of the speaker. We perceive everything, from landscape to the narrator's endless chores, through her eyes. Her narrative starts with an apology, and a description of 'how I ought to feel' but can't. The beauty of the landscape offers some comfort, seen through her own and her visitor's eyes, but it cannot cure or heal their economic struggle or her physical decline. The emotion at the end of the passage is close to despair, conveyed in the phrase currency of everyday conversation ('there, I have said it out', 'I don't know').

In both texts, narrative structure and point of view are essential to communicate meaning. In text A the narrative is event based ('And then...', 'And we had a look', 'And he recognized...'), whereas the narrative of text B is emotion driven.

▨ The final paragraphs discuss how attitudes and values are conveyed.

Both speakers — almost by definition in virtual monologues — communicate their attitudes and values clearly. In text A we know what Anna feels about the visit to Derby ('it was so funny', 'just on the off-chance'), that family relationships and history mean a lot to her ('our only surviving relative', 'my dad', 'members of the Lamb family', 'all these people...'), and that she is pleased with Fairfield Hall ('very very nice Georgian', 'very interesting'). Anna expresses her personal view even about social history ('really obnoxious [name]', 'silly dresses') but is more serious emotionally as she looks back at the visit: 'it was really strange to sit...', 'it was really really strange'. So although the overall purpose of the narrative is to amuse and entertain, it also has an expressive purpose. In this it links strongly with text B, which is entirely expressive. Frost crafts this monologue to convey to the reader the attitudes, values and emotions of this worn-to-death woman. The poem's title, 'A Servant to Servants', sets the theme of physical and emotional drudgery despite the severe beauty of the environment. Thinking of others ('I didn't make you know how glad I was') is enforced by circumstance and by her good-hearted but unimaginative husband ('He looks on the bright side of everything/Including me'). Frost harnesses the phrases of everyday conversation ('doughnuts and soda biscuits') to landscape description ('water dazzle', 'fair, pretty sheet of water') but creates a more sinister mood by phrases such as 'Dragon's Den' and 'cold chill shivered...'. The speaker's chilling sense of detachment from reality and emotion sets a frightening tone ('There's nothing but a voice-like left inside') early in the poem, which never fades.

Both text A and B use the voice of a single speaker. The spontaneous voice of Anna contrasts dramatically with the seemingly natural voice of the farmer's wife, but their attitudes and values are different, as is the use of point of view and narrative structure. Both show clearly how different crafted texts are from spontaneous texts, however similar in format and structure.